W9-AWQ-950

HARTFORD PUBLIC LIBRARY
BARBOUR-JOHNSTON LIBRARY CENTER
R01 2 48 43

Popular Library

RC
480.5
.K53   Kirsten, Grace El-
             ish
Cop.B
             Big you, little
             you

DATE DUE

POPULAR LIBRARY

BST   DISCARD

BIG YOU little YOU

separation therapy

GRACE ELISH KIRSTEN, M.A.

and

RICHARD C. ROBERTIELLO, M.D.

THE DIAL PRESS
New York
1977

A portion of this work first appeared in *Cosmopolitan* in different form.

Copyright © 1975, 1977 by Grace Kirsten and Richard C. Robertiello

All rights reserved. No part of this book may be reproduced in any form or by any means without the prior written permission of the Publisher, excepting brief quotes used in connection with reviews written specifically for inclusion in a magazine or newspaper.

Manufactured in the United States of America
First printing

Library of Congress Cataloging in Publication Data
Kirsten, Grace Elish.
  Big you, little you.

  Includes index.
   1. Psychotherapy. I. Robertiello, Richard C.,
joint author. II. Title.
RC480.5.K53   616.8'914   76-45427
ISBN 0-8037-0563-8

This book is lovingly dedicated to
Little Lynn and Little Susan, free, happy,
zestful—and to the joyous Little in each of us

—The Authors

Contents

TABLE OF DIALOGUES

Table of Dialogues

Table of Dialogues

ACKNOWLEDGMENTS

We are deeply grateful to all those who believed in and worked so faithfully with this new technique. It was through the hundreds of dialogues produced by so many people that we were able to watch the process of Separation Therapy evolve and crystallize into a practical, workable technique.

We want to give our special thanks to the work of the Monday Night Group, through whose efforts and enthusiasm the concept of *Big You/Little You* was born, nurtured, and brought to full fruition, and to Rita Rush for her very special contribution.

We also wish to express our thanks:

To members of the Tuesday Night Group, who helped us by their perseverance and cooperation;

To the group of volunteer women who, without any previous psychological background, encouraged us by the successful way in which they adopted and began so quickly to benefit from the technique;

To our capable secretaries, Peggy Ribbecke and Ethel Beckley, for their patience, good humor, and tireless efforts in helping prepare the manuscript.

To Ms. Joyce Engelson, our editor at The Dial Press, who by her insight and well-placed suggestions, as well as her enthusiasm for the concept of the book, served as our guide, mentor, and good friend.

—The Authors

Introduction

Why am I not enjoying life more? Why am I bored so much of the time? Nothing seems like fun anymore. And if I'm not bored, I'm apathetic or depressed. Life seems like an endless repetitive routine. Sometimes I feel as if I'm just going through the motions, waiting around until I die. And yet I'm so afraid of dying or even of growing old. Why do I so often seem cut off from my feelings? I don't even know what I want. If I had a blank check, I wouldn't even know what to fill in.

Why am I so afraid of people, even a salesgirl in a store? I'm always hanging back, afraid to speak up until a person comes over and shows he likes me first. Why am I so afraid of making a mistake and being criticized? I'm always monitoring my words. I'm afraid to come right out and say what I feel because I think people might make fun of me or get angry. Why am I always knocking myself . . . thinking I'm not as smart or as attractive as someone else? Why do I always feel as if other people are more knowledgeable or capable, or have more social graces, that I'm the misfit at the party?

Why is it so hard for me to get out of bed in the morning? Why don't I turn my work in on time? Why can't I manage money better? Why don't

I enjoy my family more? I'm always annoyed or bitter or angry about something. My spouse and I spend more time bickering than enjoying one another. Sex is routine and dull between us.

Why do I dawdle until the last moment before I start studying for my examination and then feel terrible because I'm unprepared? How come when I'm at a party and should be having a ball, I worry about what's going to happen at the office the next day? Why is it that even when I'm making love I'm thinking about whether I'm doing it correctly? Why do I seem to waste money on things I don't need, and then not have it for what I really want? Why can't I ask my boss for a raise when I know I deserve it? Why can't I follow through on anything?

I just can't seem to put it all together. I feel as if I'm not in control of my own life. I'm pushed around by events, but never feel as if I'm in charge of what happens to me. I'm always the cog in the wheel, never the hub. I'm always a follower, never a leader. I don't organize my work properly, my social life, my finances, my time. Things just happen to me. I never make them happen.

Is any of this you, some of the time, or too much of the time?

If so, you are among those of us for whom something probably went wrong during our childhoods, so that we are functioning in this vaguely discontented, unsatisfying way. It is generally acknowledged that the basic thing that usually goes wrong is that the child feels he or she is not quite accepted by his parents, that he is unloved, or that he is not worthy of being loved. Your parents may actually have loved you very much, but for many reasons they were unable to make you feel it, or feel it deeply enough. So if you find yourself suffering negative, destructive, hurtful feelings, or acting in self-defeating ways, you can be sure that you had enough experiences in your early childhood—up to the age of five—when you needed special love, support, and nurturing that you felt you were not getting. The love may have been there, but if you didn't feel it it's the same as not having had it.

These feelings of not being loved enough, and therefore of not being lovable enough, not quite making it, can manifest themselves in many different ways. If you observe any group of five-year-olds playing in a kindergarten or a playground, you will see that each child, even at this early age, behaves and reacts in a distinctive way:

2

One seems very shy and withdrawn, another warm and outgoing, another very frightened. One seems to need constant attention from the teacher, another runs around and is consistently disruptive. Still another is destructive; he throws down what another child is building, or may deliberately push him and even hurt him. Another appears cowardly and afraid to hit back when he is hit.

As we watch further we may say to ourselves, "That's the kind of little child I was. I can remember how frightened I always was, and how the other kids could bully me." "I was like that little child who hits and punches and talks the loudest." "I was shy and never talked." "I was always looking for attention and approval from the teacher." Each of us, if we think for a moment, might see himself in one of these little people and, in a flood of memories, remember the feelings of the child we were.

Yes, this "child we were," with his fears, his anxieties, his insecurities, and the pain of his wanting to be loved, thankfully seems to have disappeared into the misty past. He has gone with our growing up. But *has* he gone?

The evidence before our very eyes is that he has not. For although we may not remember that child's early feelings in our conscious memories, all of us, young or old, happy or unhappy, have unknowingly incorporated into ourselves the child we were. *And that child is as alive and with us, and is as forceful a presence, as if he were living in our household.* The very child that you were is buried within you, and even today he may be controlling the adult part of you. For when you, as an adult, are frightened, it is the child in you who is frightened, not the adult. When you appear to be angry, it is the child in you who is angry. When you are afraid to try, it is the child in you who is afraid to try. When you feel that you have to be good all the time to be loved, it is the little child within you, still looking for what you wanted so desperately when you were little. You may be living an unsatisfying, discontented life because the child in you is troubled and discontented, constantly at odds with the adult part of you.

"But," you say, "what of those people who seem to be happy and functioning well? They seem to have gotten rid of their troublesome child. How did *they* do it?"

The answer is that they have *not* gotten rid of the child within

3

them; nor is this desirable. This child who is always with us, with his latent zest for living and his capacity for feeling, is a most precious part of our personality. In successful people the child is still there, but he is happy, playful, content, and secure, rather than antagonistic, and he and the adult live in a peaceful relationship. These are the individuals who have had good parenting. At an early age these children developed a sense of worth and self-esteem by catching and feeling the love and acceptance of their parents, and the limits placed on them in a firm but loving way. We can easily pick out these people who are at peace within themselves. They are the ones whose lives seem to be well managed, whose marriages are fairly serene, whose businesses or careers move along and prosper, whose homes are orderly, whose children are relaxed and successful, who seem to have time for everything, including fun, and who, when they do have a problem, cope with it in an unhysterical, adult manner. They have had no reason to be ashamed of their feelings, or to be afraid to express them, and so all their lives they stay "in touch" with them. These are the true happy grown-ups, people who since infancy have been fortunate enough to have had a nurturing environment in which they felt loved.

"Oh," you say, "if only it had been different for me as a child, I too would be happy, enjoying my life and enjoying being alive."

"Oh," you say, "if only I could, I would go back and change that child to a dynamic, unburdened, real child so that now I would be a dynamic, free, real person."

The authors of this book are saying to you that that chance now is yours.

The technique described in this book will show you how you can be aware of the child within you, how you can bring him out and re-educate him so that he feels loved and secure. Using this technique, you will be able to change the child within you to a freely functioning child, so that you will be able to become a freely functioning person.

The technique is called Separation Therapy, and its description and application are the substance of this book.

1

Separating Out the Child in You and the Adult in You

History is replete with conceptualizations of man as split, as divided into different parts. The traditional religions divide man into the *good* and the *evil*, influenced by God and Satan, saint and sinner. Some philosophical systems divide him into the *thinking* or *cognitive* part and the *feeling* or *affective* part. The split that caused Eugen Bleuler to coin the term *schizophrenia* (literally, split-mind) was between the *thinking part* of man and the *feeling part* of man. Sigmund Freud divided man into *id, ego,* and *superego*: the instincts, the executive, and the conscience. More recently the Gestalt therapist Fritz Perls would have his patients split themselves into whatever two parts of any conflict they could and conduct a dialogue between these two opposing parts. Eric Berne and the Transactional Analysts split man into three parts: the *Child,* the *Adult,* and the *Parent.* The English Object Relations analysts tend to split man into the *Child* and the *Adult.*

Recently, in fact over the past ten years, there has been an increasing tendency in the field of psychology to focus attention on a child that resides within the adult in us, to try to isolate the functions that belong to him from those that belong to the adult.

Until now the splitting of the child from the adult has been a metaphor, a theoretical and philosophical idea. This theory has been promulgated with success by several writers in the field of psychology, so no one, including the authors, could possibly claim credit for this idea as his own. In science, with the growth of a general body of knowledge, it is not unusual for several people to begin to look at a subject in similar ways. And often they feel as if *they* have made a significant and original discovery, only to find that a colleague has come upon the same idea at approximately the same time. So it was within the framework of this general view in the field—the adult and the child separation—that a philosophical and theoretical milieu was created out of which the developments in *this* particular book evolved.

HOW IT STARTED

And so it was that during one of her group therapy sessions, a patient of Mrs. Kirsten's began to describe himself in terms of a split between the Child in himself and the Adult. He talked about this split not in a philosophical manner but in very concrete terms: a little Joey, a small child whose age might be anywhere from infancy to five or six, and Joe, his adult self, age forty-nine. He made this split very concrete, real, and detailed—not simply an idea—and began a dialogue between these two parts. Another patient picked up this idea and elaborated on it. He began to have a dialogue during many of his waking moments that were not otherwise occupied, between little Sammy and big Sam. Strange and wonderful things began to happen to him. Other patients, hearing what appeared at first to be unbelievable success stories, began to try it. The particular therapy group was composed of some patients who were functioning extremely well and responsibly in certain areas, but who were seldom in touch with their real feelings. They were often depressed, morose, totally anhedonic (never having any sense of joy). Others were immobilized and functioned quite poorly. The thing they all shared was seldom being in touch with

6

their feelings. Now they began to experience some childlike (not childish) emotions. It became easier for them to sing, dance, be playful, to begin to enjoy sex, begin to give and take and share love and closeness with mates from whom they had been emotionally estranged. And people who had been losers, who had functioned very poorly in their professional or other adult capacities, began to find a real zest for their work, began to get to work on time, to take work home with them at night, and were soon receiving rewards and promotions. To some it seemed like magic.

Now, what was this magic? Was it just another form of positive suggestion, another "transference cure," an example of yielding to group pressure to push aside neurosis or psychosis and function optimally? Well, perhaps. But these people had been in treatment with Mrs. Kirsten for years, some for many years. They had been in groups before. She had used many modes of therapy with them, including psychoanalytic approaches as well as suggestion and occasional behavioral techniques. How come they had been plodding along up to this point, improving steadily but not dramatically, and now were reporting a sudden spurt?

Mrs. Kirsten became excited by the results her patients were achieving. She shared her growing interest and the excitement of her experiences with Dr. Robertiello. They discussed them. They listened to tapes of the patients' sessions and read written reports of their dialogues between the separated Child and the Adult. They both became convinced that what was occurring was not just a coincidence, nor merely the result of suggestion. Of course, both suggestion and group pressure played a part in it. But they were strongly aware that there seemed to be a special and particular value, too, in the specific technique of this very concrete split between the adult and the child. They tried to understand why this split, this separation, with its running dialogue, seemed to work whereas other kinds of splits and techniques had failed.

The technique not only created this split but kept up a running dialogue between the two parts, the Child and the Adult, that pervaded a good part of the waking hours of the individual. All therapists know that one of the major factors in the outcome of treatment is the patient's own degree of involvement, his will and desire to change. A patient who seriously uses Separation Therapy, who spends *this* much time on it, and exerts this much effort in an attempt to change, is much more likely to achieve success.

But, even though we are presenting Separation Therapy as a new technique which may achieve outstanding and swift results, we want to be very sure that it is not regarded as some gimmick or simplistic formula. There are very excellent scientific reasons why it works, and we want to make it clear that this is so, that there is nothing magical about the results achieved. Again, even taking the enormously important factor of strong patient involvement into account, there appears to be a special value in the use of this particular split and in the continuing dialogue between the Child and Adult parts of the person.

Let us go into details of the split, and the philosophical, psychological, and psychoanalytic basis for the splitting of the individual into the child you were and the adult you are (or wish to be). If we split a grown-up person into an adult part and a child part, it isn't difficult to understand that unless this split is made very concrete and very explicit, these two parts will very likely be in constant battle with each other. Rather than a peaceful coexistence, in many people, and especially in the troubled, there will often be a state of constant struggle—even war—between them. Many of us forget the small child that is part of us. But *in all of us* there is a child that wants to be soothed, caressed, cuddled, admired, repeatedly told that he is loved, given constant reassurance that he will not be abandoned, negated, harmed, or destroyed. A child who is fortunate gets many of these responses from his mother.* Many of us, less fortunate, do not. Later on we may get some of these responses from our fathers, siblings, grandparents, relatives, counsellors, and friends. Our need for responses of this kind never ends. *Even when we have had optimum responses in childhood, the child in us always requires a continuation of them.* And if we were not fortunate enough as children to get them, our need for them is stronger and more insistent even though we grow older. There is nothing abnormal about these baby needs. A healthy adult has them in varying degrees and acknowledges them without guilt or shame.

*For purposes of convenience we will often use "he" instead of repeating "he or she." We will also use "mother" to convey "nurturing parent," while understanding that this could be the father or some surrogate.

But many of us are made to be ashamed of these needs. Our parents say, "Why don't you grow up? Haven't you been a baby long enough?" The answer, of course, is that it is all right to continue to have these needs. But we are small and powerless and ignorant. We take the disapproval of our parents and of others as gospel. So we figuratively hide this baby in a closet and sometimes we even come close to killing him. Since we do not take care of our baby in appropriate ways, he has to find indirect and inappropriate ways to express himself. He makes us mismanage our lives in many areas. He makes us pay no attention to the needs of other people. He makes us whine and complain. He makes us overeat, overdrink, take drugs, because we feel deprived and misused and ungratified. He makes us depressed, nasty, and joyless. He sabotages the adult in us and interferes with adult functioning.

But the adult does not do his part properly, either. He does not understand or treat the child kindly. He is ashamed of him. He hides him. He pretends that his feelings of fear, guilt, needing to be loved, do not exist. He starves him emotionally, and never gives this child the soothing and comforting he needs.

So we have two parts of ourselves that are usually not clearly separated or identified by us. They are constantly harassing one another, never giving to one another what each needs. This struggle is going on constantly, and usually without our having any full awareness of what is happening. All we know is that we are troubled, unhappy, and dissatisfied.

The system that we have devised to deal with this basic and universal human conflict involves, first, the individual's clearly separating out these two parts of himself, the Child and the Adult.

Simply stated, in Separation Therapy the individual views the Child part of himself and the Adult part of himself as two concrete, objective entities: an actual, objective figure of a child and an actual, objective figure of an adult. In Separation Therapy they are distinct from each other and completely separate, a figure of the child we once were, and a figure of the adult we wish to become. Separation Therapy then sets up a conscious, reciprocal interaction, an actual conversation between these two figures. This incorporates all the insight the individual may have about himself and his childhood, regardless of where the insight may have come from—other therapy, reading, or private ponderings—and forms it into so concrete a concept that it becomes a tangible, working tool.

The adult figure, whom we call Big, the adult part of ourselves, will give the child figure, whom we call Little, whatever it is the child has been needing—love, reassurance, admiration, comforting—and will act exactly as a good parent would act toward a cherished child. Through the use of the Separation Therapy, which we will discuss fully throughout the book, the Adult will be changing the Child from an unhappy, troublesome child to a free, unburdened, relaxed child. In the process, the adult will be freeing himself of the Child's destructive, negative influence, and will begin to function more and more in a truly mature, adult manner. The Child in return, happy and untroubled, can be a real child, and can give the Adult all his free-flowing feelings and emotions, the charm and joy in living which enhances the personality, and which is the most beautiful and precious part of us.

The following dialogue illustrates the way in which the separated adult can soothe and change the feelings of a frightened child. In this case the child is frightened and angry because he feels abandoned.

(Note that at no time do Big and Little exchange roles.)

Dialogue #1

BIG: You seem upset, Little; what's wrong?

LITTLE: I'm sad and mad. I want to cry and scream.

BIG: What's the matter?

LITTLE: My mommy has left me. [Actually Mommy in this case refers to his wife.]

BIG: She's still here.

LITTLE: But she's cut off from me. She's been all upset about her own mother, who is sick, and for the last two weeks she hasn't paid enough attention to me.

BIG: She can't help that. She has to visit her mother. She's in the hospital. She had an operation.

10

LITTLE: I don't care. I want her. I need her with me. The hell with her mother. Her mother can drop dead. And so can she. I'm mad. What *I* need is what counts.

BIG: I don't blame you for being mad. I can understand how you would be.

LITTLE: Big deal. You can understand. That and fifty cents get me a ride on the subway.

BIG: I know you need more than my understanding and acceptance. But let's start with that.

LITTLE: I hate her. I hate her. I need her. She always leaves me. How do I know she'll come back? She may never come back. I'm sad. I'm lonely. I'm scared. I can't get along without her.

BIG: Now there. She'll be back. She always comes back. You have a right to be mad and scared and sad and upset, but remember she'll be back. She loves you.

LITTLE: O.K. I feel a little less scared, but I still need her. What am I going to do till she comes back?

BIG: Well, first of all try to get comfort and attention from all the other people around you. And keep talking to me. I'll give you love and attention and I'll make you feel better till she comes back.

LITTLE: You will?

BIG: Yes. Whenever you feel needy, talk to me. Even if Mommy [wife] isn't here, I'm always here with you. You can always turn to me. *I* love you and I'll make up for her being away. And I'll help you reach out to other people too.

LITTLE: O.K. But don't go away. And don't you forget about me too like you do so many times.

BIG: I promise. I'll try my best not to forget about you. But if I do, you just tug at me and remind me.

LITTLE: O.K. I *do* feel better now.

The authors wish to make clear that this system of the separation of Child and Adult, and the dialogue between them, is not designed to replace other forms of treatment, but it is simple and can be applied with good results by almost any person, and by some, we believe, with rather startling results.

The authors have found that, with only a brief explanation, the technique can be applied at whatever level of insight an individual has when he begins, and can be used more and more effectively as he achieves successes and gains more insight.

And, even though this book is designed to provide the reader with insight into the scientific basis for this technique and a deeper insight into the technique itself, and though an understanding of good mental health is useful, these are by no means essential.

In this book we will elaborate on the Separation technique, and we will include throughout the book case histories of people who were in the original group which developed the technique, as well as written dialogues and tapes of people who have used the technique since.

2

Why It Works: The Theory Behind the Technique

Over the past twenty years much of the interest in the theory of psychoanalysis has focused on the development of the infant from birth through his first year of life. Many things have been discovered, some of them quite startling. One of the major discoveries has been the absolute life-and-death necessity for a great deal of physical and emotional as well as verbal communication between the mother or mothering person and the baby during this period. For instance, doctors found that in foundling homes in which the baby had had fulfilled all of his needs for food and warmth and excellent medical attention but very little emotional contact with any human being, almost all of the children fared very badly, and a startling percentage of them were actually dead by the end of the first year.

When babies are not held, talked to, sung to, played with, shown new objects, and generally responded to, they stop developing physically and emotionally, they lose interest, turn away from the world, and become especially susceptible to infections which can literally kill them. Moreover, babies need to be adored and admired. They need to see their reflections not only in the mirror but in their parents' faces. Most parents feel that their little baby is absolutely the most beautiful, marvelous thing that was ever created. They are completely unable to be objective about their own child. How often we are subjected to baby pictures by proud parents! This business of the baby being the apple of the parents' eye may have been boring to *you* but it is absolutely essential for the baby. To a great extent, the way the baby perceives himself and his body is determined by the amount of adoration he sees reflected in his parents' eyes. That is the reason many adults who are objectively beautiful perceive themselves as ugly and why many adults who are objectively unattractive perceive themselves as beautiful. The image that we have in our own mind of our own face and body is quite different from its objective representation.

But this admiration and love do not give us only a reflection of our bodies—they give us a reflection of our total selves. When our parents respond to us with love and admiration, we, as babies, not only feel physically beautiful but we feel we are nice, worthwhile, lovable people. And we expect others to respond positively to us. And in many ways this expectation does lead to our getting positive responses.

Negative expectations can lead to a self-fulfilling prophecy that in fact prevents us from getting what we want. It is very true that our expectations have a great deal to do with what we end up getting. And our expectations of other people are determined in large measure by the kind of treatment we have gotten from our parents, especially our mothers, in the first year of life. Psychoanalysts are focusing more and more of their attention on the early mother-child relationship as being very crucial to the formation of a healthy or an unhealthy person. The phrase "good-enough mother" has been used to describe a mother who, though she is not perfect, is generally positively responsive to the needs of her child. This means that she enjoys being a mother and having the baby, that she finds joy in feeding and holding and changing him, that she responds to his cries for food or warmth or companionship, that she is patient and understanding of his need to depend on her and his fears of not being able to cope without her. A "good-enough mother," however, is not just totally good and sweet and kind. She must provide a certain structure for her baby and must even give him an optimum amount of frustration. She must not do things for him that he can begin to do for himself and by himself. She must allow him to grow, including his eventually growing apart from her so that he can be an independent, autonomous person.

The degree to which the child received this good-enough mothering largely determines a great deal about the adult's character. We speak of "mother" because in the first year of life, and particularly in the early months, though the father is very important, the mother is in most families decidedly more influential. We are not implying that what happens after the first year of life is not important. As a matter of fact studies have shown that the results of bad mothering or the absence of a mother can be reversed if they have not gone on for too long. Nonetheless, early experiences in the intimate mother-and-child relationship *do* determine a great deal about whether children will be happy, trusting, loving grown-ups who expect and easily get good things, or whether they will be suspicious, angry, masochistic, withdrawn, focused on themselves and their bodies, hypochondriacal, pessimistic, and otherwise upset and unhappy people who make their own lives miserable and often others' as well.

We are not trying to blame Mom for everything. First of all, things can go wrong after the first year in ways that do not involve her at all. And even if she was not a good-enough mother, this does not imply that she did not do her very best. She may have been physically ill or she may have had postpartum depression. She may have had to work to provide food and shelter for her baby and not have had enough time to be with him. There might have been a brother or sister who was in some physical or emotional crisis that required her presence more urgently and legitimately than he did. Or, try as she may have, she may not have had the emotional capacity to love and fondle or feel joyous about her baby. She may have been given bad advice from her pediatrician about how to raise her baby. You may have been a baby when pediatricians often advised mothers to let babies cry, to feed them on schedule every four hours. We know now how damaging this is for a baby, but no one knew this for certain at that time. Also, a mother may have had a poor relationship with the father that kept her so upset that she was not able to give the baby the kind of attention he needed. In

15

other words, you do not have to blame or damn your mother if you happen to be one of the many, many people who did not get good-enough mothering. Your conscious recollections and present feelings about your mother may be very positive. If they are, by all means keep them that way. But if you are also generally unhappy, disgruntled, dissatisfied, or unable to function as you would like to, recognize that there is a good chance that something went wrong for you during that period. If enough went wrong, you may be now seeing a psychotherapist. That is as it should be. But if something went wrong but not quite enough to push you to get professional help, or if high-quality professional help is not available to you for financial or geographic or other reasons, or if you feel you would like to try this for yourself, then the technique of Separation Therapy can be used to try to fill some of the gap that was left by whatever deficiency there may have been in the early mother-child relationship.

Is it possible to make up now for something that was missed then? One answer to that is "Of course not," which is correct. But another answer, equally correct, is "Yes," if you think of repairing *some* of the damage rather than of a total reversal. And actually, psychotherapists are using theories derived from knowledge described above, and some are using techniques not too dissimilar from ours to put those theories into effect.

3

Let's Start Right Away: An Untrained Women's Group Tries Separation Therapy

Even though the technique of Separation took three years to develop in the original group, it is the belief of the authors that this technique is so valid and workable that it can be applied by any person who is truly motivated. *If you are now in therapy, there is a great chance that it will speed your therapy along; but in no way can it interfere.* Even if you feel that you are functioning satisfactorily now, we believe that this technique can help to unlock yet untapped potential. If you have no background in therapy it can still work for you, if you want it to, and if your motivation is strong enough.

This chapter will describe the brief instructions and description of the technique used with a group of persons with no background or knowledge of psychotherapy. Their experiences are presented as evidence that even with minimal understanding, almost anyone willing to make the effort can do it.

Remember, you do not have to understand immediately all the ramifications of this technique to begin to use it successfully, as will be seen in the following experiment.

At the point at which we tried this experiment, members of the original group had been in therapy for varying lengths of time and were using the Big-Little technique fairly well. All were enjoying at least a fair degree of success with it, though some were doing better than others. The steps used in the practice of the technique were beginning to crystallize, and it was at this point that we began to wonder whether people who had never had any therapy could understand and use it. Our aim was to see to what degree people who were not psychologically oriented could apply this technique to daily living. We organized a group of women who were interested in knowing more about it. The only requirement for being included was that one must never have been in therapy at any time. When we were sure of this, we started. We were surprised when, with only little knowledge, they were able to apply Separation technique almost immediately.

In this experiment, which came fairly early in the development, we did not delve too deeply into the roles of the parts of the personality—the Child (Little), the Adult (Big), and the Individual who contains both. All seemed to understand the notion of a little child within them. They realized that the Child (Little) needed an Adult (Big) to take care of it and help it when it was in trouble. We worked on these two concepts with considerable success, on a superficial level.

We began by asking each of these women if she could describe for us the kind of little girl she had been. Several couldn't remember what they had been like. We then suggested that they look for pictures of themselves when they were young, and talk to relatives who could help them remember. This worked for some. Those who, for one reason or another, could not see the child they had been were asked to imagine and describe what they thought they might have been like as children. They soon became involved in lively discussions, stimulated by those who could easily see their Little in action, and were soon able to describe what they thought they had been like as children, and how they might possibly have acted. Some pictured themselves as happy or sad, or lively or afraid or belligerent, and others saw themselves as being too good, never making any waves.

The following question was then asked by the therapist: "Would

18

you be surprised if I were to say to you that the little child you were is still with you and inside you?

"The little girl that you were just talking about is the child that you have to visualize now as outside of you. Place her outside you and at a distance of at least five feet, for then you will be able to observe her and see that she is sometimes happy and occasionally sad, or that she may sometimes be sad and occasionally happy, sometimes contented and sometimes in great trouble and angry. When she doesn't know what to do with her feelings, she needs help. She needs someone to take care of her and assume the responsibility for her very being. Only if she is outside you, the individual, and some distance away, will you be able to see when she is having emotional difficulties. Remember, she is only five years old, or even less, and cannot solve or cope with life's problems. Yes, she needs help and understanding and love, and Big is the logical person to give it to her. This you can do only if you, as the Adult (Big), are aware of her constant presence. If Big can accept this concept and make the decision to help her and take care of her, Big, the Adult part of you, becomes stronger and stronger.

"Let us remember that when Little dominates Big, Big becomes weak and ineffectual. As Big becomes stronger and takes control, Little stays in the position of the normal five-year-old, lively, loving, and full of emotion, unable to take frustration and unable to make decisions. And let us also remember that Big (the Adult) cannot discard Little even if she thinks she has forgotten her, for the Child is, and always will be, an integral part of the person. So if you feel it is worth the effort, you can learn how to take care of her and help her. You can help her become the normal little five-year-old with spirited emotions that are healthy. But even this healthy child needs the understanding help of Big (Adult), especially when Little is troubled, as she so often is. As the child you were is given love and understanding, complete and total acceptance, Big (Adult) will be able to help her become a source of great joy and gratification to you, the individual."

These women were then asked, "What is your little girl doing right now?" They had to stop and think for a minute, and then one woman said:

19

Big: She's sad.
Therapist: Ask her why she is so sad.

The woman asked the question, and at first there was no answer from Little. But after a time Little began to talk rapidly, and all kinds of early-childhood hurt feelings tumbled out. Not everyone was able to do this at first, and even the woman herself was surprised by what she was hearing.

Several other members talked about their own Child (Little) and were able to recapture the early emotions of their little girl. One discovered that her Little was angry; another that her Little felt unworthy and inferior. Another felt unloved. All were shocked at the intense degree of emotion that was buried in their Child. It is not certain to what degree each accepted this technique, but in a short time almost all were able to work with it. They kept reporting on how they were using it. At first Little and Big were not sharply defined in their own minds, but as Big practiced talking to Little, each day found their progress more exciting to them. The women seemed to enjoy the challenge of being able to help and make decisions for a five-year-old, who had never been able to make them for herself. Almost immediately they began to understand that *the instant* the individual felt depressed, inadequate, frightened, or anxious and didn't know why, she must talk to the Little Girl and ask her what was wrong. Little, quickly and without thinking, would pour out her uninterrupted feelings. Then, knowing what was troubling Little, and wanting to help her, Big was able not only to help Little but to strengthen herself as well as she assumed the role of the Adult (Big). With little instruction, and knowing little of the refinements of the technique, they were able to do this almost immediately.

The following are some of the experiences reported by the members of the group as they began to use the Big-Little technique in all phases of their daily lives:

"I don't talk to her. I just see her out there needing my help, and I want to give it to her. I know my Adult has to be in control all the time. So often I would have fallen apart if I had not gotten in touch with the Child. My Child is so sad. I think there is no fun in me."

This woman, with no previous therapy, was just beginning to try to see her Little Girl and was having some difficulty with it. However, several days later she said, "Last night my Little Girl was happy. I'm afraid to let her out and be too happy. I can see her now, but she is sad and very afraid."

Somewhat later she said, "My Little Girl was angry. My Adult said, 'Don't be angry.' I talked to her and wouldn't let her sulk the way she always had when she didn't get her way. She got her happiness through me, the adult."

[Therapist's comment: Her early use of the Separation technique shows that she is beginning to separate Little from Big, which is the first and basic task. At this point she did not quite understand the role of each, though she did understand it fully as she persevered.]

Another woman said, "I was in a bad mood and I turned to my Little Girl and asked her what was bothering her. She told me that she was unhappy because nobody loved her. I made it clear to her that I love her, and that I will always take care of her, and that she doesn't have to worry. I find that when I talk to her and take care of her, I am really talking to myself and taking care of me, and this makes me feel good."

Another woman described how she was discovering her Little: "I began to picture my Little Girl, and what I was like. I know that I loved my father and he loved me too. I would sit on his lap, and I was so happy. I was Daddy's little girl. When I was three years old, he died. I must have missed him and been angry because he left me. All I know is that my mother tells me that after his death I became rebellious, extremely difficult, and very emotional. Sometimes I don't like the little girl I was.

"But now I can see her out there and cheerfully say, 'Hi, Little Jane, how are you?' And I can see her cheerfully replying, 'I feel good,' and so we both feel good.

"When I was little my mother pushed me around and made all my decisions for me, and I was afraid to tell her what I thought or even answer her back. Then I married a man who pushed me around. He appeared to be so sure of himself, and he seemed to know exactly what he wanted. *Now I know that I married someone like my mother.* My mother treated me as if she thought I was stupid. He treats me as if he thinks I am stupid, and that is the way I always felt about myself. All my life I thought I was stupid. But I know it is my Little who was given these feelings, and I, as the Adult (Big), am now able to straighten out her misconceptions."

Members of the group were soon able to use the technique in practical everyday situations.

Mary, married, mother of one son, went to visit her sister, who was living with their mother. As Mary entered the house with a friend, her mother verbally attacked her and insulted the friend. Mary was hurt and angry. She could not understand why her mother still continued to humiliate her as she had done all her life. It is interesting that, although Mary had been a rebellious kid, she was still afraid of her mother, whom she had never in her whole life answered back. This day, the more her mother talked the more furious Mary became. She said, *"I saw my Little Girl out there, suffering as I had suffered when I was little.* It took a lot of guts, but I turned to my mother and said, 'Mom, I'm a big girl and a married woman. . . . When I was little I had to take it, but I don't have to take this kind of abuse from you anymore. I'll be better off if I don't see you.' "

In this incident, without a dialogue, Mary quickly became aware of the little girl she had been, who was now suffering intensely. And she thought, *"No one will ever hurt you again. I will not permit it. I will take care of you always."* In the process, Mary felt strong and peaceful and in control. She had assumed the responsibility for taking care of and helping her distressed Little Girl.

When Mary phoned several days later to talk to her sister again, her mother answered as if nothing had happened, and said, "When are you coming over to see me?"

And Mary answered, "As long as you treat me the way you do, I'm better off if I don't see you."

This was the first time in her life that she expressed her true feelings to her mother, because she was now protecting her Little and she was not afraid. And again she felt separate, strong, and adult.

Janet, another of the women in the same group, called and said, "I have got to tell you this because it is so good. The other night my husband and I went to a dance. Since I am fifty years old and haven't danced in a long time, I was shy about getting up. As I sat there and watched the youngsters doing all the modern dances, I became more and more shy. I wanted to dance very much, but sat rooted to my chair. But my Little Girl wanted to dance. She wanted to get up on that floor, and I knew it. She kept saying, 'I want to dance. Take me up to dance.' After a little time and an internal battle, I said to her, 'Come on, Little, let's go. I promised you fun tonight.' *My little girl had a ball, but what was even more important, I had the time of my life. I couldn't have cared less what anyone thought.* I rocked and rolled and just let myself go like I've never done before."

(Being aware of her Little Girl's desire to dance and have fun helped Janet make the decision. She realized that there was nothing wrong with what Little wanted. She was ready and willing to assume responsibility for taking care of Little's needs.)

One woman reported that she had had an interesting Big-Little dream:

"I dreamed that I was working in my kitchen preparing a lot of food all at once. I noticed a little girl sitting on the edge of the table watching everything I did. She was laughing, smiling, and talking to me. I told her to sit there and enjoy herself—which she seemed to be doing. When I awakened I was happy, for I had enjoyed the dream."

(This was her happy Little Girl, watching and enjoying what Big was doing. The feelings of the Child frequently appear in one's dreams.)

Gradually, as the women began to better understand the separation of Big and Little, they were encouraged to talk out loud to their Little at least once during the day when possible, and were asked to write down the dialogues that took place.

The following are some of the dialogues submitted to the therapists.

Dialogue #2

BIG: Why are you so sad?

LITTLE: I'm lonely.

BIG: Why are you lonely?

LITTLE: I want my mother. She's never with me.

BIG: Where do you think your mother is?

LITTLE: I don't know. All I know is she is never here when I want her, and I need her. [The Child is beginning to express strong emotion.]

BIG: But your mother is always home.

LITTLE: She always has so much to do. She doesn't even look at me, and I want her to love me and take me in her arms, and she won't do it. [The Child is expressing this angrily.]

BIG: Your mother wants to be with you, but she has to take care of your sick brother.

LITTLE: I don't care. I want her to hold me and kiss me and tell me that she loves me. [The Child becomes more upset.]

BIG: It would be nice if your mother could do that for you, but she can't. But I know how you feel, and you will never be lonely again.

LITTLE: Why?

BIG: Because you will always have me and I will always take care of you, and you will never be alone again. [Big is reassuring Little.]

LITTLE: But I want you to love me all the time, and tell me.

BIG: I will always love you.

LITTLE: Promise? And you won't forget about it the way you always do?

BIG: I will love you always. I promise to remember that you are over there, and that I am here, but we are always together. [Big is giving Little reassurance that she will always take care of her. This is what Little constantly needs and wants.]

Dialogue #3

A woman's dialogue with Little after telephone conversation with her husband, from whom she is separated:

LITTLE: See? He's calling me. I told you he missed me.

BIG: On the contrary. You know I have to read between the lines with him. He doesn't miss you or me. He's just feeling lonely and sorry for himself.

24

LITTLE: Well, why not? Here he is, a fifty-year-old man, living in an apartment without even a regular shower and sleeping on a mattress on the floor!

BIG: So what? That's the way he wants it. Don't you remember when I was going to his apartment and he tried to show me how self-sufficient he was, heating ravioli in a can and telling me how delicious it was? Does that sound like a man who is trying to make up with his wife?

LITTLE: Oh, that is his pride—just his pride.

BIG: You mean false pride. There is a difference.

LITTLE: Besides, I miss my dog. I want to see him and play with him, and I can't do that if you don't talk to him.

BIG: I miss my dog too, but we both know I had to leave him with my husband because I was working all day and it isn't fair to leave an animal tied up in an apartment when he can have someone to take him out during the day.

LITTLE: You don't love that dog, or you would do anything to get him back.

BIG: As much as I love him and miss him, I have to love and respect myself more, and that's why I won't allow myself to fall into that old trap again. Now let me finish what I'm doing and I promise I'll play with you later, because you know that I love you very much and there isn't anything in this world I wouldn't do for you.

All this was possible in fewer than five formal sessions with the therapist. A year later, with no further formal sessions, when the therapist again contacted the women to ask how they were doing, she was most interested and pleased to learn that all of them were still finding the concept extremely helpful, and were using it, though mostly in a limited way.

These are some of their comments:

1

I am now divorced, and am finding this Separation technique especially helpful. Without realizing it, I am using it all the time. A couple of months ago, I went to a nightclub with a friend. The music played "The Way We Were." This was a song that my husband and I had danced to often. Tears welled up in my eyes. I could feel my Little

25

Girl taking over. Being aware of this, my Adult took control and I was able to manage well for the rest of the evening. I find myself gaining much strength.

2

This Separation technique helps me very much in certain situations. When I am having an argument with my husband, I quickly say to myself, "This is my Little Girl and his Little Boy fighting." When I realize this, I see my Little Girl out there. Although I do not necessarily talk to her, seeing her and knowing that I have to take care of her brings the Adult into focus, and I latch onto the Adult and our arguments are not prolonged. It is most beneficial to me, and I use it often.

3

This woman had only three sessions, and a year later, when the therapist called to ask how she was doing, this is what she said:

This technique has changed my life. I know that I have to take care of my Little Girl. Nobody ever took care of her. I must now, and I want to. I am tired of having her take over and control me. She can no longer scream or fight, because my Adult is now in charge. By this time she knows that she can trust me. For her this is important, and for me it is even more important to know that I can do it. All my life I was incapable of assuming any responsibility.

During this past year I got a selling job, and last week they made me manager of the store. Now I see that I am capable of assuming responsibility, and this makes me feel good inside, and it makes my Little Girl look up to me. She knows that I can take care of her.

I want my Adult to be in charge a good part of the time, but it is important for me to let my Little Girl come out and shine. She makes me feel exciting, especially when I feel the need to play and have real fun.

I find that my Adult is not always smart; but now that I am aware, when I make a mistake I know that I don't want to make the same mistake twice.

I was always afraid to speak up and give honest feelings, afraid to express opinions for fear of an attack from someone who would make me feel stupid. I am no longer afraid. I say what I have to say and feel that I can manage ticklish situations, should they arise.

I am growing less needy all the time, and this is making me into an adult. Seeing my Little Girl out there makes me happy, and I love my Adult, who is in charge so much of the time. For me, this technique has been very important.

4

This woman had five sessions in the group.

This Separation technique is making my life easier. I used to fly off the handle, especially when I thought someone was trying to intimidate me. A good friend of mine and I were having a conversation about beauty. When she was finished talking, I said, "To me, beauty is not the clothes you wear or the cosmetics you use. To me, beauty is deeper than that. It is something that shines through the person, not the clothes alone."

She went home, and didn't call me for more than three weeks. So I called her and she lashed out at me, saying that she didn't like the way I talked to her. I made her feel stupid. But my Adult was in control, and I said, "I'm sorry if I made you angry. I didn't mean to, but I was only giving you my honest feelings and we don't always have to agree." I felt as if I had handled it well.

When I hung up I realized how upset I really was, and I turned to Little and said, "Stop it. Don't be upset. You are acting the way she did. I can manage this situation, so you forget about it." And I felt better.

I apply it especially when I get angry.

Each of these women felt they would like to learn and read more about the technique.

These experiences indicate that the technique's explanation can be successfully applied on a superficial level, even with minimum explanation.

There will no doubt be questions at this point, which we hope will be answered as the reader continues through the book and puts the technique to work.

CASE HISTORY

Sandra

Sandra came into therapy at the age of thirty-four. She was anxious, tense, rigid, compulsive, and guilt-ridden. She had many fears—fear of open spaces, fear of traveling, as well as fear of death and hell. As time went on, she revealed additional fears—fear of sex, fear of leaving the house, fear of closed spaces, elevators, subways, crowded places, tunnels, heights; fear of being driven in a car, fear of walking alone, fear of being alone, fear of rejection, and fear of knives. She said, "I am afraid of knives. I tie ropes around the kitchen drawers at night because I am afraid I will kill my baby."

Hers was an extremely traumatic childhood in which she felt completely rejected by a hostile father who beat her up at the age of eighteen, a masochistic mother, and two unkind sisters who had each other and didn't need her. She was the youngest in a family of eight children. Sandra was accepted only by an older brother who loved her and to whom she was much attached.

Having been brought up in a hostile, angry, strict Polish family in which all sorts of limits and restrictions were constantly being placed on her, she grew up full of fear, hate, and anger, which she repressed.

At the age of nineteen she met Chuck, and married him at twenty-one. Chuck was inarticulate and incapable of showing feelings. His family rejected her completely, yet dominated her, continuing where her father had left off. Though she was very angry with her husband because he never protected her from the attacks of his family, she never expressed this hostility.

Sandra had her first anxiety attack when she started going out with Chuck. Soon after marriage, because she developed a fear of traveling in trains, she was forced to give up her job, which she loved and through which she received much recognition and praise.

After a year of therapy, she began to feel less afraid and even walked to the park with her baby son and a friend. "I used powerful suggestion on myself and felt great." But the following day, when

29

she had to leave the suburbs where she lived to go to the city, she could not go without taking a pill. She dreamed constantly, and her dreams revealed her childhood fears of rejection and very great insecurities. Her dreadful nightmares involved constant punishment for supposed childhood transgressions. She had many anxieties and guilt feelings involving childhood sex play. As her guilt feelings were lessened, she began to make progress. She released a great deal of hostility toward her father and her husband. She fought overtly with her sisters but also fought easily and almost constantly with every member of her family except her brother Tom, whom she loved because he loved her and gave her so much recognition.

Sandra understood that she had manipulated circumstances, through her fear of being alone and her other anxieties, to keep her husband at home when he was not at work. Actually, she feared that he was gambling. When she learned that he *was* in debt up to $15,000, she was furious with him for lying and deceiving her for so many years. She wanted to leave him, but she was too emotionally weak to make a move. So she stayed with him, went to work, and helped him pay his gambling debts.

She again became depressed because she felt that she could no longer trust him. She lived in constant fear of having a nervous breakdown like one of her sisters, who had been committed to a mental institution at an early age. Because of her intense feelings of insecurity at this time, Sandra was more dependent on her husband than ever.

With time, she began to understand how masochistic she was, for during her lifetime she had been exploited by many people close to her. She continued to express additional fears: fear of the dentist's office, fear of separation from Mama; but most prevalent was the fury she felt toward her husband because of his betrayal of her and her young son and the deprivation they were forced to suffer because of his compulsive gambling.

Her brother Tom, from whom she received complete acceptance and love, made her feel somewhat secure. Gradually, under therapy, she began to lose her fear of traveling, but was still afraid to go any distance from home. She still had anxieties about visiting her sister, who lived on Long Island, and about passing the mental institution in which another sister had been confined.

But she began to develop a great deal of awareness. She realized the terrible background from which she had come and wanted to release the memories so that she could begin to live. She also began to understand that certain of her friends appeared to be detrimental to her; and even more important, she stated that her friends castigated her because she allowed them to. She was truly getting in touch with her masochism. She realized that she punished herself whenever she appeared to be enjoying herself. With this new awareness and the use of positive suggestion she was able, at times, to control her masochism. She said that her mother was ignorant, illiterate, and never went out alone. "I don't want to be like my mother. I want to be like my father. I'm masochistic like my mother. I don't want to be masochistic and die like my mother did, so full of hate and anger and guilt feelings. She had no choice. At thirty-six, I'm getting to be just like her—grumpy, unhappy, snappy, angry, and gloomy."

She said she felt like a child but knew that she was an adult. She was unable to manage her reality, for whenever her security was threatened, she acted like a child. She stayed with this insight and was constantly becoming more aware.

As time went on, she was able to get out of the house. She began to sell cosmetics very successfully and began to show signs of developing confidence.

She continued to be suspicious of her husband, who she thought might be gambling again, and there was real estrangement developing between them. At times she still felt rejected by him, her friends, her sisters, and her father.

Problems with her sisters continued. They all seemed to be vying with each other for her father's money. She was afraid that her sisters would influence him to disinherit her. She was still afraid that she might have a mental breakdown, but it bothered her less frequently. Though she became emotionally stronger, she was still aware of her dependence on her husband and father. She said, "I live in the past but have no ambition for the future." Though Sandra felt this way, she was developing a terrific amount of drive and very much more confidence. She went from one selling job to another. She developed many new interests. She was becoming extremely capable and efficient. More recently she got a job in a local store and loves it. She is getting a tremendous amount of recognition from her associates and her bosses, who have just made her manager of the store. She travels alone, by car, a considerable distance from home and is happy with this development.

She still has problems with her husband, Chuck, and complains that she has no fun with him. He tells her he doesn't know what love is. She is afraid he can't be cured of his gambling and wonders how sick he really is. She is not sure of how to act with him; if she is sympathetic she fears that she will weaken him, and if she is strong she fears she may be too rejecting.

However, she is less angry with him and more accepting of him as a good friend with problems of which she must be constantly aware. At the same time she is establishing relationships with some dynamic and interesting women. At this point she is socializing well and with real self-esteem.

Sandra, over a period of years, continued to develop more insight, more awareness, and more self-esteem. On an ego level, she developed capabilities in many areas. However, when she became emotional, she regressed and still operated on an immature level.

When Sandra had been using the dialogue in our Separation Therapy for some time, she made the following observations:

For years I have been talking to the Adult in me . . . so that the Adult is able to accomplish more, is more realistic and practical at times. And I've come a long way. I came out ahead—*but no one ever taught me how to handle this Child.* I was aware of the Child and knew that the Child acted up when I got upset, but I didn't know how to handle her. I know now that it is really like talking to myself when I talk to her, and I'm getting the answers out of myself. My attitude is changing toward my husband— catering to him more instead of constantly being angry and hostile. I am managing better with both my son and my husband. I do what I have to do for them lovingly, but I do not sacrifice myself. I know that I have to grow and so do not get guilt feelings when what I am doing is helping me. The minute I don't talk to Little Sandra, I get messed up. No one ever said, "I love you, Sandra," when I was little. Tom, my brother, was the only one who let me know that he loved me and I loved him. But he never said it. Little Sandra needs a lot of love and I have to give it to her.

Until you work with separating for a while, you can't make the separation, but I am learning. I am much more aware of Little Sandra, and I'm learning to have fun with her; and at the same time I'm also learning to be a more practical adult. When I forget her and I am not aware of her presence, I still get messed up. My husband said, "I'm getting a message from you. You are getting prepared for a life without me." I said, "No, that is not so. I just want to keep growing."

I have come so far. I can mingle and talk to people . . . and understand them so much better because I know that many people operate on a childish level a good part of the time. It takes the anger out of a situation, because I know that I cannot reason with a child. I can only deal with his emotions. But with people who are acting or thinking on a mature level, I can reason. Then I do—but I must always be aware of the level *I* am operating on before I act or speak. It is again, for me, that split second of awareness.

My life is very interesting. I came from a background where I was brought up to be silent and to hide everything—fear, anger, joy, all my emotions. Then I married and nothing really changed. I never felt as free as I feel right now. I'm free from fears of other people influencing my Little Girl, and no one can intimidate her because I have found ways to protect her so she is not as fearful as she was. After all, she has never really had anyone to love her or protect her. But as I keep proving to her, by experience, that I can do all these things for her, she loses her fears and learns how to trust me not by my talking to her but by my doing for her. That is very important to me and to her.

I have a high feeling today and I know it is because my Little Girl is happy and I as an adult feel the rewards of taking care of her. She doesn't try to punish me when I take care of her. It is only when I ignore her that she punishes me, and only when I allow her to take over and try to handle adult roles that she becomes completely frustrated. And that leads to anxieties, depression, anger, and withdrawing. I must remember that.

It's ironic how much I always depended on my husband; now I look at him in a different light. He is good for me because he allows me my freedom to grow and he supports me. My son has a good father. But my Little Girl doesn't need him and that is what is important to me. Using this technique takes the anger out of me because I try to understand that his Little Boy is often in command, so he doesn't know how to converse with me at times. When he is acting as if he is four years old, how can he? If anyone rejects my Little Girl or wipes her out, I will be there to help her. I will tell her how much I love her—how beautiful she is. I will always protect her and allow no one to abuse her.

The following are some of her very many dialogues:

Sandra/Dialogue #4

This dialogue shows incomplete separation as yet, but is interesting in that it asks an important question that patients sometimes ask:

LITTLE: I don't like having you talk to me and me to you. I'm afraid it will drive us crazy.
BIG: Why? What makes you think that?
LITTLE: Your talking to me and my talking to you is like we are two different people in one body—like a dual personality or *Three Faces of Eve*. Do you know what I mean?
BIG: But we are not crazy and I understand what you are saying. Everyone we know has a little Child in them for humor and fun. The Adult helps the Child function, and goes and gets for the Child, and teaches the Child and supports the Child and cooks for her, reads to her, buys for her, and most of the time speaks for her. We see it every day. It's really simple. It doesn't make you crazy. What we are doing is only for normal people.
LITTLE: But what about the crazy people who say they hear voices and do crazy things and say someone told them to do it?
BIG: They are sick people. We are not sick and we are only listening to each other. The Adult handles the situation all the time, as soon as she can. Crazy people can't do that. They hear strange voices and can't turn them off. Believe me, we are not crazy, because we talk to each other, know what we are doing, and can stop at any time.

Sandra/Dialogue #5

In this dialogue Sandra gets in touch with the deep fears and emotions experienced by Little at the age of five. "Talking to the Little Girl takes pressure out of me and gives it to the Little Girl."

BIG: What's the matter, Little?

LITTLE: I'm scared. I can't help it.

BIG: I understand how you feel and I love you. I don't want you to have pains in the stomach. Please don't punish me like that. I love you and I want to make life easy for you.

LITTLE: I'm nauseous.

BIG: Why?

LITTLE: You don't understand. I am afraid of people.

BIG: Why?

LITTLE: They won't accept me.

BIG: Why?

LITTLE: I am stupid.

BIG: No, my dear. You are not stupid and everyone you wish would accept you really does—from kids to adults to even old ladies. They all accept you and I accept you.

LITTLE: You don't. You didn't even understand the pain in the stomach. I'm going back to when I was a little girl.

BIG: Please tell me about it.

LITTLE: Papa was making a delivery and he parked near a church. He took so long and I was alone in the car, and I was so scared. I was afraid he wouldn't come back for me. You weren't there to watch me. Nobody cared. He didn't care whether I wanted to go with him or not. I had to go. I always had to go and act as if I wasn't afraid. I was so scared and I wanted to go home. I got out of the car and started to run. I was little and the buildings were so tall and I didn't know which way to run and I kept running around and around until I found the drugstore on the corner. I was so scared. I lied to my mother. I told her a bum was trying to open the door to the car and she believed me. But my father continued to take me on deliveries with him anyway, and I kept getting pains in my stomach. I couldn't protect myself. I couldn't cry and I couldn't show that I was scared. No one comforted me. No one cared. I don't like to think about it. It makes me withdrawn and quiet like when I was very young.

BIG: I understand and I love you. You have me now. I'm all grown up, hard and strong and very capable. I can take care of you. You can talk to me and I will comfort you. I will hug you and kiss you and I will understand your fears. I am a strong person. And remember, we are detaching emotionally from Chuck, and this will make me even stronger and smarter and more capable than I've ever been. So I can take care of you. You'll feel my presence and know that I am always here, and I will take you everywhere with me. *You'll never be abandoned.*

LITTLE: But what if it doesn't work?

BIG: It will work. I'm sure it will work. I love you, Little.

[Therapist's comment: Sandra has gotten in touch with Little's very early painful, frightened, fearful feelings of abandonment. Big, who is separated, is reassuring Little and assuming the responsibility for taking care of her, which is the Adult role.]

Sandra/Dialogue #6

In this dialogue Little is reliving a traumatic experience. The reader will notice that the separation is not complete.

BIG: Why do you have a stomachache?

LITTLE: I'm afraid of going on the train and being alone in the city.

BIG: But you won't be alone. You'll have me.

LITTLE: But you'll walk out.

BIG: No I won't. I really never did.

LITTLE: But Chuck was always with us and he helped bring you back home. Who are you going to talk to?

BIG: I'll talk to you silently.

LITTLE: I'll listen. But we'll be all alone, and I'll be afraid.

BIG: No we won't be alone. We'll take a cab or a bus or the train. No matter how we go, I'll be with you. We'll go by cab. I've decided to treat you. Does that make you feel better?

LITTLE: I can't trust you. You may walk out on me and run through the streets and not catch your breath. Then I will die.

BIG: I promise you that I will not run through the streets. With all that I have learned, I can handle it. With all I've learned about handling other people, I can definitely handle you and me.

LITTLE: I won't have fun with you.

BIG: Yes you will. There's always humor in us; you know that.

LITTLE: Mr. H is dull.

BIG: Yes he is, but I may have to support us someday and get us a lot of things. For this we need money. I'm really doing this for both of us, so we can have pretty things and a nice apartment and money in the bank. Then you won't have to be afraid of Chuck's gambling. We'll have a job and a nice one. So tomorrow is not only for me. It is for both of us.

[Therapist's comment: Big is getting stronger, though she is still partially unseparated and still says "us" and "we" instead of "you" and "I."]

Sandra/Dialogue #7

BIG: Come on, sweetheart, we are going out.

LITTLE: I like that. (Little and I get down to that car of mine and she sits on the fender so that I can see her and speak to her. This may sound silly, but since I am a new driver it helps me to drive carefully.)

BIG: You can come with me. I'm going to work now. There are going to be times I have to speak up and defend myself and times I have work to do, and I will make all the decisions, but remember, I love you all day long and I will never abandon you again. Wherever I go, you will go with me.

LITTLE: I like that.

BIG: Let's sing, sweetheart.

LITTLE: (sings)

BIG: That's it, let it out real strong! (I notice when I am in touch this way my days are good and the sales receipts in the store are good, and all the women and everyone I come in contact with likes me. Because I can understand my own Little Girl, I can understand and handle children and adults who act like children.)

[Therapist's comment: In reassuring the Child that she is making the decisions, Sandra is assuming the Adult role and is separated from Little.]

Sandra/Dialogue #8

In the following dialogue Little and Big are not yet completely separated. Big should be saying "you" and "I," not "we," in order to maintain the separation.

BIG: You seem angry, what's the matter?

LITTLE: It makes me angry that Chuck can come and go without me. I want to go too. I resent all this damn work. I hate it. Let's have some fun instead of all this damn music and psychology s——t. I want love and I want fun—to be happy. I never had it. That's why I was always undernourished and skinny. I was starving for love, and who could eat food when I was always knotted up?

BIG: I know, Little. Let's try to remember when we work together that no matter what we do we're not feeling alone and we do have fun and laugh and relax and enjoy our food. We can do that again. Just you and I. We don't have to share our fun and inner peace with anyone but ourselves. O.K.?

LITTLE: Well, we'll have to give it a try. I'll try.

Sandra/Dialogue #9

In the following dialogue Big and Little are only partially separated. Basic early-childhood needs for love, cuddling, and closeness are expressed by Little, and Big, in touch with these feelings, is able to give her what she needs.

BIG: What's wrong?

LITTLE: I have a stomachache.

BIG: Why?

LITTLE: I'm afraid.

BIG: Why?

LITTLE: You ignore me.

BIG: I'm sorry, but so many things came up I had to handle in an adult way. I was confused. *You were trying to take over, and yet I had to act the adult.* It was all too much, but I'll tell you what: I'll listen to you all day and if I don't hear you, don't be angry. It's not because I don't love you. I do feel sorry for all that you've been through. It's because I forget. You remind me. O.K.?

LITTLE: Will we have fun?

BIG: What is fun to you?

LITTLE: Going and doing and laughing.

BIG: Okay, we'll go and do something—even a long walk.

LITTLE: A long walk is for you, not for me.

BIG: Well then, my love, what's fun for today?

LITTLE: I don't know. Relax so I won't have a stomachache. You know, I remember coming home from Aunt Ann's house and she was rubbing your stomach. You always had stomachaches, and she cuddled you. You don't cuddle me enough.

BIG: I cuddle you.

LITTLE: Yes, I know and I love it. That's why I want to be close to you right now.

BIG: I understand so well, and I'm glad you told me.

LITTLE: I never had anyone cuddle me, except Aunt Ann. Where can I get more cuddling?

BIG: Well, let's see. If that's all you want from him, I'll tell Chuck to cuddle you more.

LITTLE: That's right, and remember when he was cuddling you before you got out of bed? I loved that feeling.

BIG: Beautiful! I'll hug people more often.

LITTLE: But then I'm embarrassed by body contact.

BIG: Why?

LITTLE: They will think I want sex—both men and women.

BIG: We won't care what they think as long as I give you what you need. Come on, we can be selfish too, you know. F——k the world and what they think.

LITTLE: O.K. I love you. You take care of me.

BIG: I love you too, and I will always take care of you.

[Therapist's comment: Big is giving Little what she wants and needs.]

Sandra/Dialogue #10

This dialogue shows separation. The Child is staying in her five-year-old role and the Adult is very much in control of herself.

BIG: What's wrong?

LITTLE: I hate passing that hospital. It reminds me of my sister Betty.

BIG: I understand. I don't blame you for your fears, but you will never have a nervous breakdown like her. I will take care of you and allow no one to expose you to that ever again, because I love you. You're angry at Chuck. Why?

LITTLE: He's stupid. He knew he wasn't allowed to make a wrong turn with the car. He's still taking chances. He wants to mess up my good time. He knows I get nervous.

BIG: I know how you feel and you have a right to be angry, but Chuck's Little Boy made that turn. Don't worry about having a good time. I will allow you to have a ball. No one can spoil your good time. I won't permit it!

LITTLE: I love you.

BIG: I love you too . . . more than anyone in this world. Tonight you and I are going to a party that is important to me. But there will be times I must take over because it's important. But I promise you, you can sing and dance and giggle and have fun and let loose all night. I want you to have fun. This is a night you can have a ball with people and make them laugh and sing and dance just like you want. You're going to have such a good time. Just remember at times I must take over and be in charge, but then I will allow you to have fun again.

[Therapist's comment: Big is encouraging Little to have fun, but she is also putting limits on her.]

Sandra/Dialogue #11

The following dialogue again shows complete separation, in which Little and Big stay in their appropriate roles.

BIG: Did you have fun today?

LITTLE: I would have had more fun with Helen. She understands me better.

BIG: I understand you, and I'll try even harder to work on my head because you and I together are great. You give me youth and life, and I take care of the practical end for all of us. O.K.?

LITTLE: I love you.

BIG: And I love you—very much.

Recently Sandra said, "I have never been as content with life, as able to cope with life, as I have been since working on the separation of Big and Little."

4
The Beginning

It will provide additional understanding and insight to the reader, we think, if we describe Separation Therapy as it was developed in the therapy group where the concept was first realized.

As with so many other valid concepts in analysis, this one came out of working with a person in treatment, and out of the interaction between that person, the therapist, and the group. For some time Mrs. Kirsten had been encouraging her patients to get in touch with their innermost feelings, to examine and understand the emotions which, through their therapy, they had come to realize originated in their childhoods. She urged her patients to practice consciously "staying in touch" with these feelings of anger, or fear, or embarrassment, or withdrawal, etc. She urged them, once the origin of these feelings was realized, to try as much as possible to manage these emotions and their own actions in as sensible, practical, and adult a way as they possibly could.

Discovering the Child, Little You

The entire Separation technique began with the concept of being aware of the Child within each of us, and this is where the novice should also begin. This is necessary because, as we will see, the process of getting in touch with and understanding the Child, Little, is a necessary preparation for the mature adult. Little You, as a concrete concept, was discovered, as we have said, quite by accident.

One evening during one of the group sessions, Joe, forty-nine years old, who had been in therapy for some time but never able to get in touch with feelings, said, "A very strange thing happened to me this week, Grace. I was thinking about something you had said to me about my childhood, and was talking to myself, when it suddenly seemed to me that I saw a little boy standing in the corner." Mrs. Kirsten asked him to describe the boy and he continued, "He was very quiet and afraid, and he told me that he was lonely and sad." And she said, "Just like you when you were a little boy." He continued, saying, "Yes, that's just the kind of a sad, abandoned little boy I was." With that he burst into tears. For the first time, he was able to get in contact with his early childhood feelings of abandonment and loneliness. She suggested that he try further to talk to this little boy and find out more of what he was feeling.

Sam, another member of the group, who had also been in therapy for some time, and who had also found it extremely difficult to get in touch with any feelings but anger, said, "Joe, I like that little boy idea, and I am going to try to talk to *my* Little Boy this week." When Sam returned the following week, he admitted that he had tried but that he didn't like his Little Boy and didn't want to talk to him.

Therapist: What's the matter with the Little Boy?

    Sam: He's a horrid kid. He's a coward, so afraid of everything. He's mean and full of anger. He hates everybody and everything. He never smiles. He never laughs. He's a mess. His father hated him and he hates himself.

Therapist: I don't think he is a horrid kid. I think that he is just a kid who has been misunderstood. Sure he is angry, but he has a right to be angry. His mother smothered him and his father always

found fault with him. All he ever wanted from them was to
make him feel loved.

Sam: I still don't like him.

Therapist: Keep trying to see him and to help him, if you can.

Sam: How can I help him?

Therapist: He needs to feel loved. Try to give it to him and talk to him,
if you can.

Gradually other members of the group, with encouragement from
the therapist, tried to get in touch with their own Little Child, the
child each one of them had been. It was slow at first, and took several
months, because the technique was evolving, and both the group
and the therapist were still feeling their way.

There was much discussion of the Child, whom the therapist
referred to as Little. She emphasized again and again that Little was
full of primitive anger and feelings still unresolved from early childhood; that although Little could be relaxed and happy at times, that
same Little also had tremendous needs which were not being
fulfilled, and for which he was extremely agitated and upset and
unhappy. When something unpleasant happened in the life of the
adult it could trigger a strong, even violent, reaction in the Child.
When that happened, Little, with all his powerful, uncontrolled
emotions, would overwhelm the individual—so that at times it was
impossible for the individual to function.

The therapist worked with the group to train them to develop that
split second of awareness; to be conscious of the emotions going on
inside them the instant they were experiencing them. At this instant, the individual was to separate these feelings from himself and
place them on the Child.

Separating the Child

The therapist emphasized that the only way the individual could
control Little was by imagining Little, the Child, with all of these
troubled feelings, as outside himself and separated by a distance of
at least five feet. This separation, the therapist realized, was the most
essential part of understanding and managing the Child. It was
essential because, with a visualization of the Child and all his prob-

lems standing outside the individual, the individual could then be objective: He could then stand off and observe the child as he behaved in all his moods and feelings—angry, sad, happy, withdrawn, anxious, playful, etc. Being objective, the individual was then able to help the Child, who might be suffering from all kinds of troubled feelings. The individual could solve the child's problems and do so without being emotionally involved. Being able to separate allowed the individual to think objectively.

This concept of putting the Child outside, separating him, came slowly, but the therapist continued to urge the group to *see* the Child, to see Little outside themselves. With the therapist's continual encouragement, the group practiced placing the Child outside themselves, and at the required distance of five feet—*to their left if they were right-handed, to their right if they were left-handed*, the Child being below them and on the weaker side. For some this process was easier than for others, but all were eventually able to do it.

The therapist urged the group to try to understand their Little Child, who might be suffering. She wanted them to be constantly aware of what the child felt and needed. She emphasized that the Child needed what any child needs, especially a child who is troubled and overwhelmed by emotions he cannot understand or control. He needs to feel loved and accepted. He needs to be reassured and made to feel secure. He needs to be relieved of guilt. He needs to be made to feel that he will always be taken care of. He needs to be free to be happy.

She instructed the group to *talk* to the Child five feet away, and tell him what they themselves had wanted to hear when they were little. She also asked them to express love and reassurance to the Child in order to take away his feelings of insecurity, anger, and unworthiness. She told them to try verbally to give their Little Child the petting and coddling every creature needs, and which can change an upset, unhappy child to a more relaxed, secure, accepted child. She suggested that they try to use expressions like the following, which every child needs and wants to hear:

I love you—I love you more than anybody else!
You're the most special little girl or boy in the whole world!

44

I will always take care of you; you will never have to worry about anything.
You only have to have fun, and not worry.
Tell me how you feel, and I'll solve the problems for both of us.
You're cute and fun, and I want you to play and be happy.
I love you—you're my special, adorable darling!

By showing love to Little, protecting him, and assuming responsibility for him, each would have, the therapist felt, a clearer understanding of his Child. This could work toward helping his Child to become a happy Child, one who would be a light, bubbly, relaxed, calm spirit; one who would not only not interfere with the functioning of the adult, but who would infect the adult with his own delight and make life fun for both of them.

What the individual was to stay aware of was that the five-year-old child needs someone to protect him from his own damaging feelings, and that he wants someone to assume responsibility for him and his very existence. Once the individual is ready to accept the responsibility for the well-being of his Little Child, he is accepting responsibility for his *own* well-being. *He is making the decision to take care of himself.*

Talking to the Child

The therapist suggested that each person in the group practice talking to his Child at least once a day.

This talking to the Child is what in the Separation Therapy technique is called the dialogue. In the previous paragraphs we described what has taken place in order to establish the foundation for the dialogue: There needs to be acceptance of the concept of the Child, awareness and understanding of him in all his aspects, and an attempt to communicate with him. But once these things have had their seasoning period and are firmly established, the dialogues between the Adult and the Child take place easily and become more and more clear-cut and useful. The dialogue, with examples, will be explained in detail in a later chapter, but for now it can be described as an imaginary—or better still, an imagined but actual—conversation between the individual and the separated Child. It can be verbal

or written, although writing down the dialogues, especially at the
beginning, is found to be more effective. The conversation usually
starts with a question like one of the following: "What's the matter?
You seem to be upset." "What's bothering you?" "How are you
today?" With practice, the child will express what he is feeling, and
the individual, thinking objectively, will talk to the child, soothe
him, and assume responsibility for him. A brief and typical dialogue
might go as follows:

Dialogue #12

BIG: What's the matter, Little Boy? You seem upset.
LITTLE: I don't want to go to work today. Too many problems—I can't
handle it. [The Child is expressing the feelings the individual has
inside. But now, with the Child out and the feelings expressed, the
individual can be fully aware of them and can deal with them.]
BIG: I know how you feel. [The individual gives sympathy to the child
and admits that he understands the feelings, which he does, on an
intellectual level.] But it isn't your problem. You're only five years
old. I can handle all the problems in the office today, and you don't
have to be worried. All you have to do is relax and have fun
. . . and just keep telling me how you feel. [The individual frees
the Child of responsibility—which is more than the Child can
handle—and reassures him that the individual is assuming the
responsibility for everything. He relieves the Child of his tension
and encourages him to relax. A relaxed Child is easier to keep
separate, separation being the essential condition which allows the
individual to function as an adult.]

The reader need not hesitate to start practicing using the dialogue
even at this point. The more practice the better. Nothing dangerous
will happen. If the dialogue becomes puzzling or upsetting, simply
stop.

The group reported various experiences with trying to visualize
their Child and talk to him. Those of the group who were highly
motivated made the time to practice every day. One sat the Child
next to him as he went to work every morning, reassuring him and
telling him to relax and that they would both enjoy the day. Some

greeted the Child in the morning and promised to take him along all day and let him have fun just watching. However, there was still a tendency in all the people in the group to talk to the Child only at those times when the Child was causing the adult trouble in the form of upsetting feelings or actions. It is important to know that the Child is with us even when things are running smoothly, and needs love and recognition during these peaceful times as well. The Child always wants to know that the adult is there giving him the love, recognition, acceptance, and protection, the emotional environment, every child wants. Those of the group who eventually did talk to their Child daily developed a deeper awareness of him and his needs, and moved ahead more quickly. And so it is important to hold these conversations—dialogues—on a continuous basis.

Resistance

But for a long time some patients were not able to accept the idea of their Little Child. They were unable to accept that it was the Child in them who was causing all the feelings of upset or unease. They were not able to visualize or talk to the Child in an effort to air those feelings and deal with them. Between sessions some forgot completely about the Child. Others practiced taking him out and talking to him only with the encouragement of the therapist and the other group members, and then only reluctantly.

All of these people were in conflict about changing, that is, starting the process, and were resisting, mostly without realizing it.

Some resistance is to be expected in greater or lesser degree, but the reader should bear in mind that with too much resistance the technique will not work effectively. Some of the reasons for resistance will be explained more fully in a later chapter, but the reader should do all he consciously can to overcome the initial impulse to resist.

Maintaining the Separation

But gradually even those who could not accept the concept right away began, with practice in the group, to be aware of the Child within, separate Little out, and attempt to communicate with him.

They began to realize that the Child embodied all the feelings which had been bottled up inside them for so long, and the early dialogues were of a very dramatic and epic nature:

Dialogue #13

BIG: What's the matter, Little? You look so unhappy.

LITTLE: I am unhappy and I'm angry. Why did you keep me locked up in the closet for so many years? I wanted to come out and I wanted to have fun, and I wanted to be loved and you didn't pay any attention to me and I hate you. [The above tumbled out with real, angry, hostile feelings.]

BIG: I didn't know you were there, and I don't blame you for being angry. You have a right to be. Do you want to tell me how angry you are? [At this point, Big is trying to get Little to release angry feelings, if possible.]

LITTLE: I sure do. I hate you, and I'm angry at your father and mother because they weren't good to me.

BIG: My father and mother loved you.

LITTLE: Maybe they did, but I didn't feel it. I thought they liked my brother better than they liked me. So I'm angry and you kept me locked in that closet and I'm angry because I was locked up so long and you were so mean to me.

BIG: I'm sorry. I didn't know you were there. But I will be good to you from now on and give you all the love and friendship and help you always wanted and never got from anyone. [Big is giving Little the reassurance which is so important. He should do this over and over again.]

LITTLE: I don't believe you. You'll forget about me again. [Little is still angry—still does not trust Big to take care of him.]

BIG: I may—but if I forget, tell me again and again and again until I remember. I want you to give me all your feelings. I'm not a mind reader. I only know what you tell me. So keep talking to me. Tell me everything. I want to know you and love you.

Gradually, with practice in the sessions, each member of the group began to be more aware of his Child, and to visualize him and communicate with him. But consistently, everyone in the group reported times when he was unable or made no attempt to take the Child out and talk to it. These were always times when the individual was having problems with which he could not cope. The therapist began to realize that it was at these times, when the individual was in trouble and functioning poorly, that the Child had been allowed to slip back inside the individual, had become reincorporated into him and was taking over. At these times the individual was apparently not able to separate the Child out and maintain the separation, as is illustrated in the following exchange between the therapist and a patient:

Therapist: You seem very quiet, Frank.

    Frank: I didn't want to talk. I'm lousing up all over. I antagonized one of the bosses today, and I didn't make the phone calls I was supposed to, so I don't think I'll get those orders. That's going to make my boss mad—and I'm taking it out on Roz. I was vicious to her and she spent the day in bed, sick.

Therapist: Were you able to speak to Little, your Little Boy?

    Frank: I haven't spoken to him for days—I'm too angry. . . . I don't want to speak to him. I don't care about him. I can't talk to him. I'm just angry.

Therapist: You know it's really your Little Boy who is angry. He's in control and he's the one who's lousing up. Why don't you try taking him out and talking to him?

    Frank: I don't think I can. I don't want to.

Frank's Adult had been completely overwhelmed by his Child, who had taken over so powerfully that Frank was helpless to thrust Little out of him and keep him out.

The therapist realized that it was imperative that the individual be constantly aware of what was going on inside him. He would then be able to make use of this instant of awareness to separate the Child, with all of his troubled feelings, and place him outside himself. But now the therapist realized that to maintain progress the goal had to be to keep the Child separated constantly, using a consistent, determined effort. However, for this it would seem that the individual would have to function consistently as a strong, mature adult.

But was this not the kind of mature adult which the therapist—

like all therapists—works to develop, from the beginning of therapy? Was this not the mature adult which takes so long to develop and which requires so much motivation to achieve? Would it have to take that long?

Yet here, in the group, some were very much involved with their Little Child and were working to take care of it. They were struggling to act in an adult way for the sake of this Child. It was almost as if they were into the role of being their own therapists, so that instead of the therapist interpreting and nurturing the individual's childlike feelings for one hour a week, the individual was taking care of those feelings himself at any time, twenty-four hours a day.

Could this be a motivation to induce the individual to speed his own maturing process? Could it be, as Mary explained in fighting back against her mother, "I couldn't fight my mother for myself, but I can do it for my Little Girl, who needs me to protect her."

But then, as Sarah expressed it, "I want to protect my Little Girl and to talk to her properly, but I don't know what to say. How can I be an adult to my Little Girl if I have never been an adult before?"

A good question, thought the therapist. How indeed?

In order to help the Child, the individual needs a strong Adult.

Was there an essence of an Adult which could perhaps be separated out of each individual, just as the Child had been separated out?

The Adult—Big You

The therapist began to examine the concept of the Adult with the group, using the technique which had been used in examining the Child: Could they visualize their adult selves? Did they have a mental image of themselves as adults? Could they see themselves in their daily roles, and if so, how did they look?

Strangely enough, where their Child, Little, had been for the most part vivid, the group was vague and noncommittal about their personal mental image of their Adult. A few said they could visualize themselves, but for the rest the adult image seemed to be hazy.

For one patient, Frank, seeing his Adult seemed more difficult than for the others because he was unusually flat and withdrawn. The following exchange between Frank and the therapist took place:

Therapist: Why don't you try to visualize your Adult, Frank?

    Frank: I can't even see his face in my mirror.

Therapist: Keep trying and see what happens and let us know.

Some time later the following ensued:

    Frank: I can see the face but not the body. I can see the face with a kind of pleasant expression . . . but it's not really pleasant. It's a grin. And I still don't see the body.

Frank resisted getting involved; but seeing the progress of others and wanting so much to function on a more efficient level, he kept trying. In his case, he had to work hard to stay with it, for he was constantly tempted to withdraw. Although at times he did fairly well, unless he was making an effort to stay with it, the Adult slipped away from him. But with determination and practice, Frank eventually succeeded in seeing what appeared to be his very wobbly Adult.

The therapist felt that what might be happening when an individual was not able to see his Adult was probably that he did not want to see his Adult, for the same reason that he had not at first wanted to see his Child. He was not proud of him and did not like him well enough. He was in a sense denying his Adult, just as he had denied his Child.

Since it seemed more difficult for the individual who was now able to see his Child clearly to see his Adult sharply defined, the therapist asked group members to try to *visualize their Adults* in some activity —any activity in which they felt they could perform well, or even fairly well. At first they protested that they did nothing well, but after a short time and a little discussion each began to remember little areas in which he had had feelings of real success.

One, though very needy, mentioned his tennis game. Another, basically needy and withdrawn, could easily see himself as the successful and efficient salesman he was at those times in which he operated efficiently and was in control. One woman, especially needy and dependent, saw herself cooking a delicious meal in the kitchen, where she was in complete control. Another saw herself as a fairly capable secretary—and still another, quite immature in many areas, was able to see herself successfully teaching her classes. Each seemed to have at least one area in which he or she felt some strength, even though much of the time they were childlike and dependent. So the group spent some time discussing at least one thing that each did fairly well. They admitted that at those times they felt strong and in command, like adults. The group focused on these adult accomplishments and feelings for quite a while. Each member of the group concentrated on evoking the feelings of confidence and stature he experienced when he was proud of his performance:

> *Mary thought of herself winning her achievement award.*
> *Jack kept in mind that he had met a high goal in commissions that month.*
> *Dan saw himself as the new supervisor for his district.*
> *Ruth kept repeating, "I was first on the list; I was first on the list! I'm somebody!"*

The therapist suggested to the group that whenever they were in situations where they felt inadequate or ill at ease, they try quietly to snap on these mental pictures of themselves, and the feelings of achievement and confidence. And each slowly became aware of a fleeting feeling of maturity in which he felt able to stand tall and energetic, and in which his voice expressed itself with conviction and strength. He could not necessarily maintain it for too long a time, especially at first, because the tendency is for these feelings to slip away when the Adult is overwhelmed by an unseparated Child. But as he began more and more to see himself in successful situations, and to feel the accompanying emotions, he was able to maintain this adult feeling for longer periods of time.

Then the therapist urged the members of the group to practice, just as they had done with the Little Child, staying in touch with these adult, confident feelings of which they were becoming more aware. And slowly an image of an adult began to crystallize.

Gradually, with the Child now separated out and quite well established, the group began to shift its emphasis from the Child to concentrating on the Adult. They talked about it, they visualized it, they had the Adult carry on daily dialogues with the Child.

The group, and the therapist, began to realize that all the work with the Child was really preparation for the growth of the Adult.

The Child had to be acknowledged, understood, and handled, but it was the Adult who was to do the handling, after all. The adult, Big, would not only be taking care of the Child but would forever after be in charge of directing the individual's successful life.

So, if the Child had to be an objective entity, personified and separated in order to be helped, why shouldn't it work to make the Adult an objective entity as well?

Separating Out Big You, the Adult

The therapist suggested that now each member of the group concentrate on *separating the Adult, taking him out of the body of the individual.*

It took an exercise of the imagination, similar to that they had used with separating the Child out, for the group now to separate the Adult. This involved many searching questions:

> *Where do I place the Adult in relation to the Child?*
> *Where am I?*
> *What do I do while my Adult and the Child are having a dialogue?*

The group discussed this, and after several weeks a member of the group said:

> *Betty:* I can see my Adult talking to my Little Girl.
> *Therapist:* Like two people outside of you?
> *Betty:* Yes—it's as if they are each at the end of a rigid arrow, coming out of me . . . one on my left and one on my right. Only I still don't understand what *I* am doing in the middle.

Ultimately, with the experiences and the insights and the suggestions of the group as a guide, the therapist worked out a mental triangle to help in the separation.

The Triangle

The Adult is to be placed above, on the stronger side of the individual (his right side if he is right-handed), and the Child is placed

53

below, on the weaker side of the individual—each at least five feet apart. The individual is at the apex of the triangle, watching each of them, seeing that each *stays* separated and in his proper role. The individual is to be the activating force in the dialogue:

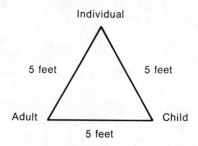

With the concrete concept of the triangle to work with, the individual can see his Child and his Adult clearly separated. He can keep each in his particular and important role. He is the one who activates the dialogue, sees that it is carried out properly, and terminates it when indicated. In the process, and with each success, big or small, the Adult grows stronger and more mature.

Questions Asked by the Group and Answers by the Therapist

It will be helpful to examine some of the questions which were asked by the members of the group as they progressed.

Q: If at the beginning Big is weak, how can she give support, love, and understanding—and the right answer—to the Little Girl?

A: When you first separate, you may not have all the answers as an adult, but as the separation is maintained the Adult grows in her understanding and handling of reality, and as she matures in this process she will be most helpful to Little.

Q: How can I be sure this will work for me?

A: The degree of success in using this therapy depends on the degree to which the person is motivated to change.

Q: What is the advantage to the Little Boy or Girl in being separate from the Adult?

A: In being accepted as a Little Boy separate from the Adult, Little is permitted to function as a one-, two-, three-, or four-year-old, and cannot be belittled for operating on that level. He can be loved and accepted with all the weaknesses of a little boy—and can be helped by the Adult, who is standing by and objectively evaluating Little's need for help.

Q: What are the advantages of Big being separated from Little by a definite space, five feet, between them which neither can enter?

A: In this separation, Big, not overwhelmed by Little, is permitted to operate on an adult level. The space helps to remind us that we must keep Little separated out. As Big continues to operate independently he gets stronger and smarter, and he develops a strength with which he is able to work through his challenges in life as an adult.

Q: How far back in age is Little able to go and still get in touch with feelings?

A: As far back as he feels he can go, even to infancy, as long as he can express feelings. The infant is to be imagined as a typical infant, except that he has the ability to talk.

Q: Does Big ever get angry and show emotions?

A: Yes, but Big gets angry on a grown-up level. He can be justifiably angry, responding to a specific injury, but he does not experience primitive, uncontrolled rage. He expresses his feelings of anger in words on an adult, ego-directed level. He says to himself, "I don't like what just happened. I'm very angry, but how can I handle it so I will come out ahead?" The Adult doesn't have to like it, but he has to cope with it.

Q: When the Adult feels gay and happy, is she incorporating the Little Girl? And who is feeling happy? At this point is there a separation or is the Little Girl taking over?

A: The Child feels the happiness, and this happiness is caught by the Adult. Emotions are transmitted and caught by one person from another. With Big and Little separated from each other, we conceive of them as two separate individuals. Big can then catch Little's joyous moods and respond to them without losing his identity or being taken over by Little.

Q: What happens when Big is rejecting and unkind to Little?

A: Little withdraws, gets hostile, and acts very much the way he did as a child.

Q: How can Big pull Little out when he withdraws?

A: Give him all the love, understanding, and acceptance he wanted as a child and felt that he never got.

Q: How can I satisfy my awareness of the lack of love in my childhood and not become masochistic through reliving early childhood deprivations?

A: It is important to relive early childhood feelings in order to understand them. But if the Adult is in touch with the fact that he is suffering needlessly, he will be prevented from staying with the suffering an unnecessarily long time. We relive early childhood feelings of not feeling loved when we go through long periods of depression, when we withdraw, when we feel inadequate, unworthy or not accepted. The Adult will ascribe these hurtful feelings to the Child, and then help to relieve the Child of them.

Q: Is it possible that, as the Child feels more love and has more faith in himself, he grows in maturity and reaches the stage where he can safely be incorporated by the Adult?

A: No. The Child part continues to operate in all of us as long as we live. It should never be incorporated.

Q: Who is the boss, Big or Little?

A: Big should definitely be the boss. He is a benevolent dictator, who provides a firm structure and continued controls.

Q: Doesn't talking to yourself and thinking you are two people mean you're crazy?

A: Not if you do it by choice for a specific purpose.

Patients' Evaluations of the Separation Technique

After some time working with the technique, members of the group were asked what they felt Separation Therapy was doing for them. The responses varied. It appears that the degree of success is clearly related to the degree of motivation and commitment the individual has to changing and becoming truly mature. Some caught on to the technique almost immediately and made continuous, steady progress. Others resisted for various reasons, but they eventually were able to break through their resistance and were also able to use the Separation technique successfully.

The therapists wrote to the members of the group and asked them in the following letter for their responses to certain questions:

We are writing the chapter on the evaluation of the technique, and are especially interested in what is happening at this time, during the summer, when we are not in contact with each other.

We would appreciate it if you would take the time to answer the following questions:

1. Can you sustain the Big-Little separation? To what degree? Under what circumstances does the Child take over? How do you manage when that happens?

2. Are you capable of keeping Little out all the time, so that you can see him and help him when he is in trouble? If not, do you know why?

3. How do you feel about Big? Is he growing stronger, so that he is in a better position to help Little? Are you able to pinpoint the conditions under which you slip?

4. Are you able to use this technique in creating better relationships in other areas: with friends, co-workers, hired help, mother, children, bosses, etc.?

5. Is this technique accomplishing anything for you and in what way has it helped you grow, if it has?

This does not have to be a success story, so please feel free to give us your honest feelings and appraisal.

The Authors

The following evaluations are taken directly from the unedited tapes and letters which the authors received in response to their questions. They reveal the differing rates of progress of each person, depending on the degree of motivation, involvement with the technique, and the stage at which the person started.

EVALUATION # 1

To answer your questions: I do not keep Little out. I rarely communicate with him at all. I am not aware of Big either. At times, I think that this whole idea is a load of b——s——t. And yet I have seen how others in the group have learned to handle their problems by using this concept. For some reason I simply have not worked at this, and I should certainly not condemn it because of my lack of effort.

[Therapist's comment: This patient resisted the technique for a long time. Eventually, however, he began to accept it, and his comments later took on a different tone.]

57

My Little says to Big, "If you are not my friend, I'm not your friend." I have decided that Little doesn't take over my role; *I* am the one who relinquishes it to *him.* I know now that I have to maintain a loving relationship and communication with him. When I satisfy his needs, he allows me to be an adult. If I do not give him what he needs and has never had, he sabotages me all the time.

EVALUATION #2

I now feel dynamic at last. I know that I can control things, because I have my Little in proper perspective. Though I see it happening, it is hard for Little to believe emotionally what is happening. I know now that my relationship with my Little has to be a loving relationship, in which I put limits on him. Big can say to Little, "You don't have to be smart. I, Big, will make all the decisions, and I will make you secure, and you will trust me and have faith in me and I will get smarter and smarter."

I didn't really believe in the Separation technique in the beginning, but I am using it all the time now and it is dynamic. I find myself functioning like an adult most of the time. When I am in trouble, I know that Big is letting Little sabotage him. I see it happening, and I don't believe what I see. I just don't believe it. At such a time I let my Adult get in charge, and I am in control.

Instead of being angry with Little as I always was, and criticizing him, I say to myself, "Why do I feel so insecure right now? It's Little making me feel so insecure." Then I as an adult begin talking, and I tell him that I will always love him and take care of him.

BIG: I love you. You're important to me. I'm going to give you everything you always wanted and never got from anyone. You'll never feel deprived again, and I will always love you and take care of you.

This is for real. Others can't hurt me. I allowed others to hurt me all my life. I did it to myself. As I am fully aware of my Little, watching him and giving him what he wants and needs, I find myself more creative, dynamic and constructive. This was a busy week for me—plugging up and solving problems—but I felt good. I am with it, enjoying things. This full awareness of the Separation technique is having a terrific impact on me.

LITTLE: That's exactly what I've wanted to hear and to feel all my life.

EVALUATION #3

This is interesting because I can be objective about myself. I can see that this makes for a much easier way of getting into feelings which I would never be able to talk about. If I can't talk about feelings which I don't want to admit to, I can place my feelings on the Little Girl. It's all right for *her* to have painful feelings and to talk about them. Then I, instead of pretending that they are not there, can deal with them.

It's an easy "How To" way, not as subjective and much easier. This technique is objective and the Adult can give himself choices.

EVALUATION #4

In a split second, I visualize my Adult self standing outside of me. He is strong, mature, and always approving of Little, the Child. And always with the feeling of "I love you, Little."

The *mere glance* at the *Adult outside of me* turns off the Child immediately and stops my Little Boy from taking over and controlling the Adult. What happens is that the Adult assumes full control and I immediately feel the difference. My body straightens up and my outlook becomes realistic, and I know where I'm at. I find now that *90% of the time I'm concentrating on seeing the Adult, rather than seeing the Child 90% of the time,* as I did when I first started using the Separation technique. I see the Adult as a mature, strong, realistic person, and in control. My problem all along was that I acted on a childish level and could never visualize myself as an adult, so I functioned as a child most of the time, without knowing it. *I visualized myself as a child.* I had *no conception of myself being adult and grown,* in most areas: at work, sexually, in relationships to all women and to strong men. I couldn't see myself in the mirror because I was incapable of seeing the adult.

Today I turn my own inner mirror on and I can see myself as an adult, but *I must still concentrate on the Adult as a loving, realistic*

individual, capable of handling everyday situations. Without this Sepa-
ration technique I feel that I would never have been able to see the
Adult on a sustained level because I could never see the Adult in me.
My career consists of coping constantly. I find that unless the individual (myself) talks to the Adult a good part of the time, the Adult slips
away and the overpowering Child takes over. Then my judgment is
bad and I cannot function efficiently. I find that at this point, though
I am good to my Child, I have to spend more time talking to my Adult
and reassuring him that he is stronger than he knows and more capable
than he realizes, and that he may not like what is happening but he
will be able to cope with it. In this way, for me it is staying in touch
with my reality and strengthening my Adult—who, incidentally, is
getting stronger all the time.

[Therapist's comment: Though this patient has very clearly defined his Lit-
tle, he is now concentrating on the strengthening of the Adult part of
him. He sees his Adult functioning quite well at certain times. But,
when he seems to be wavering, he gives his Adult good suggestions by
talking to himself and reassuring Big that he is stronger, more capable,
and brighter than he knows. This he does to help Big stay and grow
in the Adult role.

This procedure is also discussed in Chapter 7: "Staying in Control,"
in the sections "How the Adult Knows What to Do."]

EVALUATION #5

Big-Little technique has helped me at work. In my relations with all
people, and I meet many during the day, I decide in a split second
whether I am dealing with the other person's Child or Adult. If the
customer's *Child* is out, my *Adult* handles her Child. If the customer's *Adult is out*, I know that *I can reason with her* on a mature
level. This technique has also helped me be aware of which level I am
operating on before I act or speak. This Big-Little technique has made
me most skillful in dealing with people.

Little doesn't try to punish me when I take care of her and love her.
It is only when I ignore her that she punishes me. When I allow Little
to take over and let her try to handle adult problems, she completely
overwhelms my Adult. It is most important for me to stay in touch
with this.

I have a high feeling today, and I know it's because my Little Girl is happy. I, as an adult, today feel the rewards of taking care of her.

EVALUATION #6

When I compare myself now to last summer, the difference is tremendous. I feel like a grown-up. It's because of the Big-Little technique. Most times all I have to do is picture Big, strong me, and I become her. I don't even have to have a dialogue. But this only works when Little is not experiencing very strong negative feelings. At other times I have to have a dialogue and let Little get her feelings out so Big can help her in her trouble and take control. For small everyday occurrences, though, just visualizing a strong, stable adult is enough for me.

EVALUATION #7

1. Keeping Little out all the time: Unfortunately I cannot yet keep her out all the time, but I can keep her out a good part of the time. It reminds me of the way my masochism sometimes sweeps over me with no warning. Sometimes I am the Little Girl without realizing it until *after.*

2. How I feel about Big: I like myself better and even think I have some good, worthwhile qualities. This is a radical improvement for me. Big is getting stronger and more able to help Little through her crises. I slip when Big worries about something that is real to worry about. In other words, when there really *is* reason for worry, then Big has trouble comforting and calming Little.

3. Better relationships: I have a terrific friendship with D because I can quiet Little's moments of insecurity and jealousy. I am doing better generally with everyone except with my four-year-old daughter. I have the most trouble with her. I find myself being Little with her too much. My feelings for her are stronger than for anyone else in the world. I really have to sweat with my daughter to try to remain an adult (Big).

4. Helped me grow: I feel better about myself; and one *very* important thing it has accomplished: I'm *much* less angry than I used to be. No comparison. I can give love to more people more easily now. That's a tremendous accomplishment for me. I find I'm also more honest with people, in an adult way. My Little is not so crushed and insecure as she used to be, and I think that's why I can be loving and honest. It's a battle, and I find it hard to do at times. But it does seem to be getting easier as the summer goes by.

EVALUATION #8

Don't worry. This won't be a success story. As you know, I haven't been very successful with the Big-Little technique in the past. I don't see any difference in how often or how well I've used it over the summer as opposed to during the year, but I'll try to answer your questions anyway.

1. I never was capable of keeping Little out all of the time. I know that a big reason for this is that *I never tried to—I didn't want to.* Today, for the first time, I imagined what it would be like if I did practice Big-Little all the time. I felt I could do it if I wanted to, and if I did I would be able to handle anything—no more being upset— and the thought of this was very depressing. It felt very blank, like everything would be over. *I really see doing Big-Little all the time as the end.*

2. The only times I attempt to use Big-Little are when I'm having trouble. Sometimes it's too late. If I'm really upset about something, I feel like I'm all Little and there's no Big to talk at all. I'm *most successful at using the technique when I can recognize that there are two conflicting feelings in me.* Then I can work at identifying one as the Child's, and try to separate it from the Adult's. I do feel that Big is growing stronger.

EVALUATION #9

1. I know why I am not able to keep Little under control all the time. I get lazy and do not work. I push things away and Little controls Big. When I really work I am capable of reversing it, but with my lack of a disciplined approach I use a million excuses for not working—like it's hot, I'm tired, I feel overworked, etc.

2. Despite all the above, I would say Big is stronger. She takes over faster and ends my feeling of panic. The condition under which the adult slips most is still, stupidly enough, when I feel rejected by my husband. I still am far too dependent upon him, and I must overcome this.

VISION QUE

This is not a success story because I am still punishing myself. Little has been so strong for so long that part of me does not even want to give up and take control in the adult way. My biggest battle is to really want Big to be in control all the time.

I always find summer more difficult than any other season. I think I can honestly say this one has been better than any past one, despite the fact that I am totally on my own and alone a very great part of the time. *I am not lonely anymore.* I can always use Big and Little. As soon as a *feeling of loneliness starts to creep in, Big and Little have long conversations and the lonely feeling is dispelled.* This is a very positive and very good aspect for me.

EVALUATION #10

I have never felt so strong and so alone in my entire life. I realize for the first time that everyone has problems, not only me. I, like the rest of the world, have to learn to accept, assess, and then go on with constructive things. Little Susan does not speak to me much lately. I know she is much too close, and yet I am able to function fairly well. I know that if Little were really separated I would be doing the things I am doing now, but with ease and facility.

Whatever I am doing to communicate with Little, it is not working —the positive approach, the discipline approach, the love approach. She will not tell me what is troubling her, and yet she causes me anxiety.

[Therapist's comment: Susan's attitude toward her Little is too intellectual. She is at this point not able to give Little enough love. When she develops loving, accepting, helpful feelings toward Little, Little will quickly feel them and respond.]

The strange thing is that *at the same time I am having this problem, I am coping very well.* I am getting done many things that were important for me to do. I am living with the fact that I cannot do everything that I set out to do. When I get into trouble, i.e. overeating, I seem to be able to recoup almost immediately. I usually know what trouble I am having, and why, and in most cases explain to Little that she need not worry and that she is making more out of a situation than really exists.

At this point, I wonder if I am talking to Little. She is not out in front of me, but she is not ruling me either.

It is weird. I feel great and lousy at the same time.

[Therapist's comment: At this point, Susan is coping so well because she is unusually bright and capable. But were Little completely separated, Susan would be achieving on a higher level, with less tension and anxiety.]

EVALUATION # 11

1. Regarding my Little: I am so aware of what makes my Little Girl angry and what makes her happy and what makes her insecure. She gets a reaction when she is rejected and she gets angry. She gets a reaction when someone makes her feel that her Adult is weak or dumb. That, too, makes her angry. She gets jealous, and that makes her angry. She gets insecure about money, and then I help her by reminding her that, for today, I have enough.

It is such an adult world. I have to be aware enough to give her what she needs. I'm fortunate because I deal with the public, and most people are allowing their Littles to handle situations. Speaking to my boss and doing all the work involved in my job, which is multifaceted, are all adult tasks. So there really isn't much time for Little to do the things she wants to do. So I just make the time for her. Another thing Little doesn't like is what I call the "cobwebs"—things which hang over my head and need doing such as re-arranging my clothes closet, writing out checks, having to make a certain phone call, looking for something I have misplaced, sewing on a button. So Big takes over. I take a few hours and clear up the "cobwebs," and then Little can relax and play.

2. Regarding my marriage: In my marriage I feel that I must function basically as an adult simply because my husband, an alcoholic, has been taken over by his Little Boy. The actions and thoughts of an alcoholic are those of a little boy. As long as I maintain my Adult role with him, I can keep things under control for me.

3. Regarding my sex life: I feel that my sex life is a combination. *My passions and desires are my Little Girl's.* They must be, otherwise as an adult I would be thinking sensibly, and that to me is not sex. In a sex relationship you have to feel free and uninhibited, which most adults are not. You have to feel free to giggle and move and play. These are not the actions of my Adult. *My Adult encourages Little to do and say as she pleases,* and *to ask for what she wants.* I definitely know that I have a good sex life. I feel that no adult would take her clothes off—or dance nude—only the Child. So many of these actions must be the Child's. *But it is important that the adult in me guide her so it all appears as a woman.*

4. Regarding the raising of my son: I have found that by making my Adult stronger I have made his Adult stronger. He, at sixteen, can do things I still don't know if I can do. My Little Girl understands his age and has fun with him also. But I feel that children need parents who are strong adults most of the time.

I know that after many years of therapy there isn't any other answer for me but this. I have read books looking for answers, and it is amazing how so many writers come so close to this technique and then lose it. You asked me if the technique has helped me grow. I can make a long list for you, but there are just too many examples. Not only have I grown, but my *Little Girl* is *free.* That is something she has never been. She laughs, runs, hugs, sings, and dances. She's less fearful because she knows that she can rely on me and I will help. Life is fun because of her and sensible because of me.

CASE HISTORY

Jim, age forty and father of a thirteen-year-old daughter, came into
therapy because he was having marital difficulties and was exceed-
ingly anxious, frightened, and hypochondriacal. He had an older
sister whom his mother seemed to prefer, and with whom he was
constantly compared unfavorably.

Jim had been in the construction business with his father during
his father's lifetime. His father, who was a hard taskmaster and
perfectionist, treated Jim in a domineering way—so that between
the mother and the father Jim felt rejected and unloved, though he
was not always aware of it. His strong attachment to his mother
disturbed his wife very much and was causing him serious marital
problems. He was at his mother's beck and call. She would send for
him to hang her drapes, to paint her house, fix her door, etc. And
though he often didn't want to do this for her, he never said no. It
was easy to see that one of his problems involved his attachment to
his mother and an alienation from his wife, with whom he was
having real problems. He was reacting to his wife very much as his
father had always reacted to his mother: with constant bickering and
fighting. His parents were cold and unloving, not only to each other
but to their children as well.

Since Jim was either consciously or unconsciously angry at his
parents, toward whom he had never expressed anger, he appeared
to have turned the anger inward, and the anger, needing an outlet,
was punishing his body in the form of stomach symptoms. He had
pain, and often suffered from dysentery. As a result of this almost
constant symptom, he was very irritable and treated his wife and
young daughter in a tyrannical and sadistic manner.

During his therapy he began to understand that the cause of many
of his problems was his attachment to his mother, since he always
felt sick after seeing her. "I see my mother less and less, because it
is she who makes me sick. When I was first married I fought with
my wife all the time. I stopped off every evening with my father to

see my mother before I went home, and she insisted that I have dinner with them. I was unable to refuse, and then went home and ate again with my wife. I fought with my wife the way my father fought with my mother." There was much friction with his wife as a result of his mother, which he was just beginning to understand and to feel.

At one point, when the Big-Little technique was becoming crystallized in the mind of the therapist, she decided to share it with Jim, who seemed interested right from the start. It was suggested that he stay with this technique as often as he could during the day, and that he be aware constantly of his emotional reactions. She also suggested that he give the emotions that he was feeling to Little the instant he experienced them. When he was able to see Little in trouble, he could help him. After a time, Jim said, "I have reached the stage where *at the moment* I feel anxious or guilty or emotional I give these feelings to Little and talk to him. It is very important for me to then let Little pour out his feelings quickly and spontaneously. He can't wait to think. If he does, something happens and he doesn't seem able to talk. *Little's response must be instantaneous.*"

During his therapy he began to develop real skill in this technique, as manifested in the following dialogues. (It should be clearly stated that after some time he had made a definite decision to see his mother as little as possible.)

Jim/Dialogue #14

BIG: What's the matter?

LITTLE: I want to see my mama.

BIG: You're five and I love you and I know how you feel. Since you aren't old enough to make decisions I have to make them for you, and I don't want to see my mother. So I have decided not to go.

[Therapist's comment: Big is also putting limits on Little by not permitting him to make this decision. He says, "I know that I have to separate from my mother to survive. When I see her I can't function. I made the decision to have as little to do with her as possible at this time.]

Jim still has conflicts about seeing his mother, but this technique is helping him make constructive decisions on an adult level.

Jim/Dialogue #15

I decided to do some work on my books at home, which I could have done at my office. I soon discovered that I was making several mistakes. I typed a letter, made mistakes, couldn't spell certain words, and had to look them up. Little just didn't want to do anything. Big carried on the following dialogue with him:

BIG: What's the matter, little fellow?
LITTLE: I don't want you to make mistakes. I want everything to be perfect.
BIG: Everything can't be perfect. Why does everything have to be perfect? It's hard to do things right all the time. Nobody's perfect.
LITTLE: Your father wanted everything perfect, and I get scared when it isn't perfect.
BIG: I know how you feel, because I sometimes get a little scared too, but I have to be able to accept errors and correct them and make all decisions. This isn't your problem. It is mine.

Jim said, "I, myself, was also irritated by being less than perfect, but I quickly used the technique and Big took over. This technique is a wonderful tool for me. When I separate from the kid and know that I have to take care of him, I seem to be more mature."

Jim/Dialogue #16

BIG: What's the matter?
LITTLE: I don't like my pains in the stomach.
BIG: I don't blame you. It hurts and you are not comfortable. I will take care of you and give you some medicine and you will feel better.
[Therapist's comment: Instead of letting Little take over and complain and fuss, Big almost immediately assumed the responsibility of helping Little, who was in trouble.]

Jim/Dialogue #17

Jim had a dream that his house was being burglarized. He woke up very frightened and immediately carried on the following dialogue with Little:

BIG: What's the matter, Little?
LITTLE: I'm scared.
BIG: I don't blame you. That dream was frightening.
LITTLE: What will I do if it happens and someone comes in while I'm sleeping? I'm scared.
BIG: I know how you feel, and I wouldn't want a burglar to come at night. But don't worry. I will take care of you, and I will take care of the problem. I am going to have a burglar alarm system put in our house and then we will all be safe.
LITTLE: Promise?
BIG: Yes.

The next day Jim had a burglar alarm installed.

When I'm in trouble I can now quickly separate Little me from Big me. I was queasy about coming back to work after my vacation, but I realized that it was not the work but having to see my mother, who always wipes me out and gives me guilt feelings, that was really bothering me.

I went to see my mother, who has been quite ill. She asked me to put up her drapes. I said to myself, "All right, I'll do it. No problem at all." But I quickly realized that my Little Boy didn't want to do it, even though the Adult wanted to do this for her because she was sick. After I finished, she started to cry and became very emotional. This is unusual for her, for she is a cold fish. She seemed very upset and I put my arms out and held her. I could feel myself getting emotional. So I separated myself from her physically. I walked to the window and looked out and told my Little Boy that I was an adult and that I could manage. It took a few minutes for me to gain my composure and I was able to leave feeling that, as an adult, I had done some good for her and no harm to myself.

This technique has helped me accomplish more self-control and so I don't vacillate emotionally from high to low. It has definitely helped me. I'm much more aware of the relationship between Little and Big, though it is sometimes hard for me to decide at what point I'm slipping. I know that when I am getting emotional feelings I am able to bring out the Adult that controls Little, and I do what I have to do without getting guilt feelings. With this technique I am able to create better relationships in all areas—socially, where I have always had problems; at work; and with my family. It hasn't been easy for me. This past summer I had situations where I was able to test my emotional problems and my ability to control them through the Big-Little technique.

While we were in the Berkshires it rained for several days, and my wife wanted to leave and go to another area, where we could have entertainment at night. I wanted to stay in the Berkshires, because I had brought my fishing tackle and had planned to make this a fishing trip. So when my wife asked me to leave I had guilt feelings because I didn't want to go and I knew she might be unhappy. I was able to quietly say to her, "Last year we went to Paris because you wanted to go, and this year we planned this fishing trip, and I think we should stay here for our whole vacation." When I went into the fishing boat I realized how angry I was because I didn't do what she wanted and I was feeling guilty. I talked to my Little Boy and worked it out very well, and no longer felt guilty or angry. I reacted in a much more mature manner than I would have several months ago, and I felt in control and adult.

This relationship between Big and Little builds up the adult ego. At the beginning I felt self-conscious, as if I was half nuts. But I find that I have gotten more skillful as I go along. You know that for years I have had a sick stomach. This is the fourth week that my stomach has not been bothering me. I eat cabbage and everything and it is all O.K., and what is more important is that I haven't had diarrhea in all that time.

This is the best week I have ever had, and I have had no need to take any sleeping pills. I am much more relaxed.

Jim has stopped trying to get the love from his mother that he always wanted and tried so hard to earn. He now knows and accepts the fact that she has never been able to give love to him, and probably never will. . . . He is now giving it to himself through Little Jim, and enjoying the love and warmth that he has never experienced before.

This new awareness is reflecting itself for Jim in all phases of living. He is better able to relate to his wife, to his daughter, to his associates in business, and even to his mother, from whom he is more separated emotionally than ever.

CASE HISTORY

Margaret

Margaret, a comparatively new patient, age twenty-eight, had never been in therapy of any kind. She grasped the Big-Little concept almost immediately and has continued to make progress by using it.

She came into therapy depressed, unhappy, and full of anxieties. She complained of pains and aches and was constantly in doctors' offices. Despite the fact that the doctors reassured her that there was nothing wrong, she insisted that she was ill. Hers had been a traumatic childhood in which, when she was fourteen years old, her mother died after a long and lingering illness. During her mother's illness Margaret spent a great deal of time nursing her, running the household, and catering to her father. Her father took all this for granted, acted as if it were all coming to him, and showed no appreciation whatsoever. Margaret's older sister, who had been very much attached to her mother, became very ill at the mother's death. And again Margaret assumed full responsibility, this time for her sister, making all arrangements and running to the hospital constantly. It seemed to her that, as far back as she could remember, she had been obliged to do for others. She could not remember a carefree childhood—a childhood with any joy in it.

When Margaret first began therapy, she was worried and upset because she did not seem able to relate in a lasting way to any man. Although she had opportunities, she never permitted herself to get involved with anyone.

She had problems involving her father, to whom she appeared to be attached and from whom she sought praise and recognition. She tried very hard to please him, but he responded with only faultfinding and criticism. At such times, being very frustrated, she would end up in tears, anger, and depression. Her sister, when not in a hospital, fought with her and also made her life miserable. But Margaret thought this was the way it had to be. She did not understand that she had a choice—that she did not have to "take it" unless she wanted to.

Her therapist, after working the Big-Little technique with her groups whose members had been in therapy for some time, decided almost immediately to introduce the concept to Margaret, who, as has been said, had never had therapy of any kind. The therapist tried to help her understand that there are two parts of the individual, Little and Big. She explained the Big-Little concept to Margaret in the following way:

Little, who is all emotion, is no more than five years old . . . and Big, on the other hand, is very logical, practical, and not the least bit emotional. Each of us has both components within herself, housed inside the individual. Little is very needy, and always, but always, wants someone to take care of her and love her. She needs constant reassurance. Big is realistic, capable, and often extremely bright. She alone solves all the problems that Little, who is only five, is unable to solve. Let me repeat: Little is all emotional, and Big, who is rational, solves and copes with all problems.

Little, inside the individual, overwhelms Big, who is also inside, so that Big—the Adult—finds it impossible to function. Hence this technique involves taking out the Little Child, as well as the Adult, so that separated, the Adult can become aware of the needs of a five-year-old child. Whenever the individual is highly emotional, the Child is in control. When the Adult is in control, the individual is smarter, more capable, and more realistic. Each has an important role to fulfill, and each must stay in her role so that side by side they can function efficiently together.

This concept appealed to Margaret, and she was able to grasp it very quickly. They began by role playing: She was Little and the therapist was Big. Over a period of time, through role playing, she reached her childlike feelings and was able to voice freely what she was feeling at all times. And Big, the Adult, temporarily played by the therapist, was able to laugh with her when she was happy and friendly and able to help her when she was in trouble, as she so often was.

After they had worked together a short time, Margaret said, "I know now that my Little Girl reacts on a completely emotional level, and when I ask her what's bothering her it gives her a chance to release on this emotional level and she can get everything out. Then my Adult speaks to her in what is a very logical, reassuring, and calming way. What I like about it is that I can use it as often as I want to and need to. If Little is angry and does not get enough of her anger out I can talk to her again a little later and she will release more anger. If she is still upset, I can give her the chance to get it out as often as is necessary. Eventually Little lets everything out that is bothering her."

Margaret continued to make progress. She was confronting her sex problem realistically, and was slowly working things out by facing up to them. She was becoming much more adult with her father, who, sensing the change in her, criticized and demeaned her much less often. If he tried, she quickly handled the situation in such a way that he had to behave decently. She was no longer permitting her sister to take advantage of her and produce guilt feelings in her for nothing. At this point she is developing a great deal of insight. Upon returning from a short vacation several months ago, she said, "My sister met me at the plane with an overwhelming verbal attack. She was angry because she had had to take care of my father during my absence. My Little Girl started to cry because she had anticipated a royal welcome and was hurt and disappointed by this rejection. My sister's Little Girl, out in full force, screamed and carried on. I was afraid that we would get into an accident, since she was driving. As soon as I realized that my Little Girl and my sister's Little Girl were fighting, I looked at my Little Girl out there. . . . I couldn't talk to her, but just by seeing her out there I was able to bring my Adult back into control. Only then was I able to function with my sister and be completely in charge on a truly adult level, and it felt so good."

The following is a transcript of her first recording upon returning from her most recent convention-vacation:

This last vacation was a great growth experience for me. Many wonderful things happened to me and for me. I had problems which I handled easily, but one very serious traumatic incident I was able to cope with only after I remembered and got in touch with the Big-Little technique. It didn't solve the problem, but it helped me get over the hump. It helped me get through the immediate problem so that I could function. It gave me a chance to stand back from it all, look at it, and see what was really bothering me. The times that I didn't use Big Girl-Little Girl, the problems built up to a point where it was difficult for me to deal with them. It was not easy for me to talk to Little, because I had very little time alone. I was sharing a room with a friend, and was always surrounded by people. The truth was that I was so involved with the active social life around me that I *forgot about Little* and *forgot to use the technique when I should have.* I think that was part of the reason I eventually wound up having an anxiety attack. The attack bothered me even more than it should have because I had been doing so well that I really didn't expect it. I didn't know where it came from, and it came on all of a sudden.

As soon as it happened, I had a Big Girl-Little Girl talk and, to some degree, it helped—though not completely at first. It helped me get back into perspective, and from that time on I managed to struggle through the next day. But I made it, which really makes me feel good. I talked to Little so many times the next day. I spoke to her that night, and in the morning. The day I was in a panic I spoke to her every time I had a chance—and I made a lot of chances. I think that's how I got through the day—by talking to her. I was really in trouble . . . in an acute state of panic. After talking it out, I made up my mind not to sit and suffer, because my vacation was not yet over. I worked on the dialogues with Little as often as I could, and in a little over one day I was feeling much, much better.

In trying to examine her feeling of panic, Margaret decided that it was the result of a combination of things. She had telephoned her father that same afternoon.

He was very low-keyed and hardly talked to me. He acted as if, since I chose to leave him, he didn't really want to talk to me. I had hoped that he would be happy to hear from me, but he refused, as he always does, to share my happiness and enthusiasm. I found this very frustrating.

Immediately following this phone call, I went into a conference where I was forced into a confrontation because nobody else wanted to handle a particular problem. I felt that other people at the meeting should have handled it, and it should not have been my problem. So I was angry at the woman with whom I had the confrontation, and furious with the people who sat back and let me do it. I was also frustrated because the problem was not resolved, even after all the fighting. I had no opportunity to have a Big-Little dialogue at this time, which I am sure would have helped me get rid of my anger, because a very special man with whom I had become involved was waiting for me. We went for a long ride and I seemed to have calmed down, for I was happy and content to be with him, but I didn't realize that I was holding in the anger of the whole day. During dinner he gently told me that he was married. My immediate reaction was anger that he had permitted me to become so attached to him, for, at his insistence, we had spent almost all of our vacation together. I was very hurt and disappointed, and at the end of a frustrating day the anger was more than I could handle. My Little Girl panicked, shook all over, cried, and was frightened. All these problems came together before my Adult could talk to her. There was just no time. I think if there had been time for my Adult to handle one problem at a time this would not have happened.

This was an overwhelming vacation. I have never had anything like this in my whole life. It was unbelievable . . . but as I look back over it now, it seems to have been too much for me to take in. I had so much approval and recognition and love. It was overwhelming, and I don't think I was able to handle it. It's amazing how much I learned about myself on this trip. I understand that it's because I am a masochist that I had to find a way to pull myself down. I was being given too much. So many good things were happening to me that I just had to find a way to almost spoil it.

I was really going through something special for me. I loved every minute, but it was difficult for me, I guess. I was being showered with love and attention and admiration from this whole group, and special unbelievable attention from certain people. This was something I had never gotten in my whole life from anyone, in any way. I was so with it and into everything, and felt like a million bucks. My Little Girl was having a great time—such a ball—and it was coming from so many different people, males and females. I let my Little Girl come out and get involved and forget all her inhibitions. But, as exciting and as wonderful as it was, I was not able to take it all in over a sustained period of time, and I ended up in a state of panic.

The panic, with accompanying "shakes," lasted for a little over a day, and as Margaret describes above, she was able to pull herself out of it very successfully. To a large degree, she attributed it to the fact that she was able quickly to get in touch with and take out Little, to talk to her constantly. She was also able to get in touch with and able to assume the responsibility for helping Little, who was in very great trouble at that particular time. During the day she went off by herself at regular intervals and talked to her Little Girl, and it worked for her.

A party had been planned, and it just happened to fall on the night after I had been in a state of panic. I was not feeling well, and I decided not to go. My Little Girl insisted that she wanted to stay home. After talking to her for some time, I changed my mind and made the decision to go to the party. I forced myself to go, and I was glad that I did, for I was given the award for the Outstanding Woman at this convention. My Adult had taken over and I was glad that I had made the right decision for me. If I hadn't gone, I don't think I could have made it through the rest of the vacation as well as I did. And I did make it, I really did, and very well.

As we see, Margaret came back from her last vacation elated and full of exuberance about the "unbelievably marvelous time" she had enjoyed. "It was like magic." She bubbled over with a new kind of enthusiasm as she talked about it. When she remembers how depressed and anxiety-ridden she had been only eight months previously—and that at that time, outside of an interesting job, her life consisted of taking care of a demanding, selfish father, coping with an ill sister, and sacrificing herself in ways too numerous to mention —she smiles and feels good.

Margaret liked the Big-Little concept from the very start. She has always been enthusiastic about it, but she came back from this last vacation full of joy and appreciation for it and for her ability to use it when she felt so emotionally overwhelmed. Margaret feels that much remains for her to learn about herself, and she understands that each day brings with it new problems. But she feels that if she continues to stay with it and works at the Big-Little technique, she can help herself understand and resolve each of her problems.

5

The Separation Triangle: The Child, the Adult, and the Individual

The specific steps in the separation which the group developed involved the three elements in the Separation Triangle—the Child, the Adult, and the Individual. Before we discuss these steps in their technical details, it would be useful for the reader to have a more basic understanding of the nature and characteristics of these three elements, so he not only can visualize them but also have a clear view of their functions and roles as they interact with each other.

The Child—Little You

Basic to the technique of Separation Therapy is knowing that the feelings of the child we once were are still within us. These feelings are still as alive and volatile and powerful as they were when we were that child. We must now think of that child and recognize him as the child we were, with all of his own particular characteristics and needs. And we must know beyond a doubt that everything we do or feel which works against us is due not to our adult selves but to the

79

feelings and the subsequent actions of this child *we once were,* who is still crying out for and demanding the love and acceptance he feels he never had.

The word *feels* is important, because even if his parents did love him, if for some reason they were not able to convey their love to him and make him believe it, he still *feels* he never had it. So his needs are still as great as if he had not been loved.

It is not easy for most of us to believe that the child we were, with all his feelings, is hidden inside us, so it may be of help to realize and understand exactly how the child in us who feels unloved develops and is then put away so that we forget he is there—and more importantly, how he is still affecting our lives even though we do not know he is there.

As we described earlier, each of us, as an infant, needs and requires "good-enough mothering." We were born with a great potential for joyous freedom and growth, but if we did not have good-enough mothering, or feel that we did not have good-enough mothering, we begin very early to be stunted and inhibited. This begins as soon as we are made to feel that our baby needs and actions are something to be ashamed of. Our mothers may be impatient with us as infants, and may not be in touch with our baby needs for loving responses. But it is right and normal to have baby needs and to want loving responses from our mothers. We want them all our lives. We gravitate to and feel comfortable even today with those people who we feel really care about us and accept us. We want this even more when we are little because we are small and fragile, easily frightened, insecure, and dependent, full of doubts about ourselves, very very needy of comforting and soothing and expressions of love, reassurance, understanding, and direction. Parents may be giving this, but some children need even more nurturing. We want our mothers to help us over difficult times by giving without question or hesitation the support we need. We want them to say, "Are you having a hard time? Do you need some loving? Come and let me hold you." Instead, we may be punished because our parents really don't understand our baby needs, or because we are an annoyance and in the way. We may be scolded, slapped, ignored, and otherwise frustrated, when what we really want is to be soothed and mothered. Our actions may be criticized, corrected, disapproved of, our self-esteem undermined, and we may be told to "grow up," to be a "big boy."

"Growing up" in our child's mind then becomes tantamount to being accepted.

In short, we are made to feel there is something wrong with our baby selves and our baby needs. We take in the disapproval of our parents and we believe it. Baby freedom and joy are stripped away, and we become self-conscious and inhibited. We are suddenly aware of ourselves and we discover that the child we are is not likable, has all kinds of wrong feelings and wrong actions and wrong needs, is not worthy of being loved. We are helpless and frightened and very alone. We want to be loved and we feel we are not. We hate everything and everybody, but most of all we hate and are embarrassed by this child we are. We want to change him, get rid of him, deny him; we want him never to have been born—anything to free ourselves of this unlovable, unworthy self and the misery he creates for us.

The child thinks of himself as unworthy and unloved, and if he could speak might express thoughts like the following: "I'm so miserable. . . . I'm no good—they don't love me. . . . I must be bad. Maybe I'm not their child. I don't know how to be good. . . . I'm stupid. They always yell at me. They hate me. . . . I'm not good—something must be wrong with me. I'm scared. I have nobody to love me and take care of me." These are the honest feelings of a child who is suffering.

If the parent were aware of how the child is suffering and what he is feeling, he might behave and feel differently toward the child, and handle him in a way something like the following:

Dialogue #18

CHILD: I'm no good. I never do anything right. I'm so unhappy!

ADULT: You're good. You don't have to be perfect. You're only a little boy.

CHILD: But you don't love me. You're always angry with me.

ADULT: I sometimes don't like what you do, but I always love you.

CHILD: But you never tell me you love me.

ADULT: You know I love you.

CHILD: But you never *tell* me you love me.

ADULT: I thought you knew it, but if you want to hear it I will tell it to you often, because I love you very much and I want you to know it.

But if, in childhood, we do not get this kind of love and acceptance, we will still feel unloved, and will still want to lose our unworthy self and put in our child's place some child whom our parents *can* love.

So we decide we must outgrow him, which we begin to do as soon as we have awareness forced upon us, and as soon as we start to acquire accomplishments and achievements which the realities of the world force on us: going to school and all its growth experiences; learning to ride a bicycle, to swim; using proper table manners, etc. We begin to put aside the baby with all his needs, and we begin to be "grown up." We want to forget all the unhappy and humiliating times which were inflicted on us for being unworthy. We do not want to think of ourselves as being frightened or hostile or angry or so vulnerable that we need loving. We attribute these feelings to the child we were, and as the adult part of us begins to grow, we tell ourselves we are leaving the child behind.

In this way we have forgotten about and tried to outgrow the child we were, but the problem is that we have done so without satisfying his needs and frustrations. We have never given him the emotional support he needs: relieved him of guilts, admitted he has a right to be angry, admitted that he wants and needs to be loved and admired, built up his self-esteem—all the things a child needs to grow emotionally. We have simply gone on performing in the real world as best we could, while at the same time systematically concealing and disdaining, ignoring and trying to deny, the existence of the Child within us whose needs and behavior we are afraid and ashamed of.

This denying of the needs of the Child we do as completely as if we had taken an actual child away from a family and shut him up in a closet and are still holding the door shut on him. In addition to needs, there is also joy and fun and playfulness in the child, the urge to sing and dance, to swing out and be free; but all of these, too, have been smothered, and the Child is behaving as any child would who has been put into a closet—he is hungry, frightened, full of misery, tearful, feeling unloved and unwanted. But this is not all, and this is not the real danger of keeping the Child in the closet. The real danger is that we have imprisoned him without responding to or satisfying any of his baby needs and frustrations. And so, combined with the hurt and misery of being locked away and ignored, there is also furious rage and anger because he has never been satisfied. He will continue angry and enraged, vicious and irrational, until he is taken out of the closet and his needs are fulfilled. Until that time he is a danger to us because he is looking for every opportunity to push his way out, overwhelm us in a split second, and take his revenge by sabotaging the adult part of us.

And sabotage us he does:

It is the Child in us who makes us late for work;
It is the Child in us who misplaces and loses things;
It is the Child in us who can't get or hold a good job;
It is the Child in us who can't reach out and make friends;
It is the Child in us who feels comfortable only with people who like him first;
It is the Child in us who makes us feel other people are better than we are;
It is the Child in us who is ill at ease in company, who cannot think of anything to say, or fears he will say the wrong thing;
It is the Child in us who makes us late for appointments;
It is the Child in us who puts things off so we get into trouble;
It is the Child in us who leaves things for the last minute so we are always under pressure;
It is the Child in us who gets sleepy so we don't pay attention when we should;
It is the Child in us who feels bored most of the time;
It is the Child in us who makes us go through days feeling blue and depressed;
It is the Child in us who smokes too much, or drinks too much, or eats too much;
It is the Child in us who says, "Don't try. You'll never make it";
It is the Child in us who keeps our surroundings messy and untidy;
It is the Child in us who is always doing favors at the cost of his time and energy so people will think he's a "nice guy";
It is the Child in us who misreads and misinterprets or overlooks important instructions so that trains, appointments, responsibilities are not met;
It is the Child in us who argues and gives excuses when presented with good advice;

*It is the Child in us who makes us think in terms of failure, or at best
status quo for ourselves, instead of in terms of success;
It is the Child in us who makes us do the wrong thing in spite of our
good judgment;
It is the Child in us who is afraid of the boss;
It is the Child in us who won't let us do what we know is good for us;
It is the Child in us whose voice is so loud that we cannot hear our
Adult's mature voice of reason.*

If the Child in us has been very much deprived, he can be angry
enough to sabotage us in big ways:

*He can make us flunk out of school, then do nothing in its place;
He can make us miss our opportunities to choose a satisfying life work;
He can make us marry the wrong person;
He can make us mishandle our children;
He can shackle us to a habit, like gambling or drinking, that keeps us
enslaved;
He can make us contemplate suicide, and sometimes succeeds.*

He makes us do these things, and he does these things to us
because he was and still is an unhappy, unresolved child whose
feelings and needs have not been sufficiently satisfied. He doesn't
know the world is now quite different, no longer populated only by
a disapproving mother and a critical father. He thinks things are
exactly as they were when he was very little, and he is acting and
responding to stimuli exactly as he did then; but now his actions
show up in the self-defeating behavior of the adult individual.

These overt actions we have described are very obvious—we see
them in ourselves and very clearly in many of the people around us.
But the Child does not stop there. The Child also controls and
dictates all of our deep-rooted life patterns, the unconscious attitudes which govern the course of our lives. For example, we may be
having a problem with authority; this may manifest itself in fear of
our boss, our mate, or the law. Problems in this area can also result
in our being overly submissive to authority, being overly concerned
about what other people think, being compulsively rebellious, which
may manifest itself in lying, stealing, aberrant sexual behavior, or

other instances of unacceptable behavior. We may be breaking rules and consciously or unconsciously inviting others to punish us. On the other side of the coin, we may be overly authoritarian, demanding and critical of others. We may be obsessional—the mind repeatedly flooded with certain thoughts. Or we may be compulsive, pushed by unconscious forces to perform certain routine or repetitive behavior. Another area in which the Child in us may manifest disturbance is the area of competition. We may be constantly comparing ourselves to others, especially negatively. Or we may want to outdo someone so badly that our judgment becomes impaired, and the need to win may force us into behavior which is not to our long-term advantage. Or we may be so frightened of competition that we avoid it where our participation in it is appropriate. Or we may enter into it but be immobilized or inhibited from doing our very best.

Another indication that the Child part is askew and affecting us adversely is if we require constant reassurance and always feel frightened and insecure. We may need people to admire and adore us continually, and feel crushed if this is not forthcoming. We may be constantly preoccupied either positively or negatively with our appearance or state of physical or mental health. We may have a poor image of our body or of our whole self. We may express our dissatisfaction by a sense of defeat or resignation. We may withdraw from the world and from contacts with people, especially intimate contacts. We may be lacking in feeling, have no zest for life, be joyless, and feel as if we are just existing or going through the motions until we die. The sexual part of our life may be inhibited and lacking in excitement.

There are still other ways in which the problems of the Child affect the Adult. These difficulties express themselves in the Adult's inability to function, in his not being able to concentrate on any area where he wishes to apply himself. This can result in procrastination, in failure to achieve goals, in not being able to follow through on ideas, in shirking decisions or avoiding them, in letting someone else decide for him, in not taking the responsibility for the course of his life, in not being in touch with his power to influence others, in always being a follower, in constantly worrying about his performance, in having blocks in creatively fulfilling his own goals, in being unable to assert himself socially or sexually. All of the preceding indicate defects in the operation of the Adult part of the individual. They indicate that the Adult has been overrun by the Child and that the Adult has lost his autonomy and strength. Almost all of us have some of these feelings in varying degrees at times. These, in general, are the result of ways in which the Child in us is disturbed, and has sneaked in and is subverting and sabotaging the Adult.

So the unhappy relationship continues. The Adult is trying to go about his business, working and hoping for success in his endeavors, while the Child inside is waiting, ready to seize control in a split second and cause the individual to act in a childish, immature, self-defeating way. The individual is usually totally unaware that this is the Child part of him. He thinks it is his "personality," and he is not satisfied with it, but he doesn't know what to do about it except by trial and error, hoping things will get better as he grows older. But they will not, until something or someone comes along to intercept these automatic, destructive responses of the Child and to control them so that the Adult can be allowed to function freely, unencumbered, and in a mature way.

The only one who can step in and take control of the actions of the Child and change his destructive behavior to positive behavior is the Adult part of us.

The Adult—Big You

We have learned the characteristics of the Child and how he is formed; we must now understand the genesis of the Adult. It is an early progression of accomplishments which is the genesis of the Adult in each of us. It should be understood that even though the little child we were, with our emotions, had been repressed, and though he may have been sullen and unhappy, the little person was still performing in the real world. He was sitting at the table, going out to play, learning to tie his shoes, asking questions, drawing pictures, learning the alphabet. These are the early accomplishments which continue into adulthood, and even though the Adult often feels at odds with himself, he can still function very well in specific areas. This Adult, Big, as you will call your Adult in your dialogues, is the part of us which is capable, able to function, and able to cope with reality. And so, just as we must consciously visualize the little child we were, the individual must now know and be able to visualize the Adult part of him when he is functioning in an adult role. We must see the Adult, and be acutely aware of the Adult's positive characteristics, because even though we have spent a great deal of time and effort in understanding and handling the Child, the object and goal of Separation Therapy is also the consistent strengthening and maturing of this Adult part of us.

Who is the potential Adult, and what are his characteristics?

The Adult is the person we are when we are functioning at our best potential. He is calm and rational, able to function and to perform and accomplish in the real world. He is the source of all our successes and all our accomplishments, all our logic, reasoning, practicality, and stability.

We must make a strong and conscious effort to visualize the Adult part of us, just as we visualize the Child, since the two parts must use the technique in conjunction with one another. We must see the Adult as he is when we are proud of him and his conduct. We must see the Adult as he acts when he is functioning well. And we must know that in spite of how our Adult may be functioning now, he has tremendous potential already within him, only waiting to be developed. Such a developed Adult can be an assertive, well-integrated person who can cope with almost any hardship or loss or disaster in his world. He is reliable, alert, self-protective, and able to protect others. He is capable of enormous self-discipline, and can suffer all kinds of privations. He is fair and just, self-seeking but capable of great sacrifices for other people. He can work efficiently, and can be very productive and creative, to the point of inspiration. He can provide food, shelter, and comfort for himself and others. He can be kind, supportive, and understanding. He requires the support and admiration of others, but can function without it if he must. He is calm, reasonable, unruffled. He is not without emotions, except that he handles them as a strong, competent adult would handle them, on an adult level.

He can and does feel anger, or annoyance, or any other emotion, but he does not allow these emotions to rule his actions so that he is out of control. He knows that he is angry, or upset, or worried,

87

or frightened, but he will direct his thinking, and before he speaks or acts will decide what is the practical, sensible thing for him to do and say.

The Adult part of us has the potential to be very strong. The Adult can meet situations that come along in a manner that will maximize his pleasure and minimize his pain. The Adult knows that he cannot control external events or other people. He knows that sometimes things will go badly, but he knows he has to take things as they come and he has no illusions that they will consistently go his way. He realizes the future is totally unpredictable, so when things go badly he may be disappointed but he is never crushed. He merely tries to make the best of a bad situation. He stays calm. He does not panic. He is always in control of himself. He immediately sizes up a situation, and he does not let his childish emotions push him into bad judgments or self-defeating decisions. He deals with reality *as it is,* not as he would like it to be. He never avoids or postpones making a choice, nor does he abdicate his role in making decisions. He seeks and respects competent advice, but he knows that no one can make a decision that involves himself better than he can.

He is a leader, not a follower, but he can be a good follower when he needs to be. He can work with others, can respect their ideas and make his own contribution without needing to take over. He is self-initiating and self-directed. He does not do a thing because it is "the thing to do," or because other people seem to want to do it, or because he will feel guilty if he doesn't do it. He is an independent thinker. He gets in touch with what he wants and then goes after it in the most expeditious manner. Before he makes a decision he makes sure his conscience approves and he has the tools to accomplish it, or at least make a good attempt at it. He also takes the responsibility for his actions, measures what the probable consequences will be, and is willing to deal with those consequences. He is able to give up short-term satisfactions for long-term gains. He is logical, reasonable, practical, stable.

He gets a genuine satisfaction and joy out of being helpful and supportive to those who need him and to those who are not as strong and wise as he. However, this does not mean that he is a compulsive do-gooder who sacrifices his life for others. But he can be very supportive and understanding, especially to children, and he enjoys being with them. He can and likes to nurture them and to play with them. He can encourage a child or another adult to express feelings. He is patient and understanding with an obstreperous child, but at the same time he does not yield to the child's threats, or to his blackmail or extortion. Instead, he sets firm limits and provides a steady structure. He is not emotional or hostile or competitive or destructive, but always kind.

He is not needy: He can go it alone. He can get most of his rewards for himself, but he is still pleased to have his accomplishments recognized and he genuinely appreciates himself and his abilities. He can take a compliment without being flustered. He is not immodest, but neither is he self-effacing.

All this may sound as if to be adult one must be functioning constantly at a perfect or heroic level. This is not so. The adult uses his potentials in proportion to the need—daily, to enhance his life as he goes about the regular business of living, and occasionally to meet a special situation when he is called upon to do so.

In short, the Adult who is separated from the Child will function in a mature, calm, rational manner. And, if there is no basic defect such as a severe handicap, or mental or organic disease, the Adult is capable of reaching his potential and achieving a satisfying life.

It is necessary that you, the reader, keep this view of the Adult ever in your consciousness, because *it is this capable, strong part of you* that will ultimately be directing your life as well as functioning as Big in your dialogues with the Child, Little.

The Individual and His Role

We have tried to define the nature of the Adult (Big) and the Child (Little) as two parts of ourselves. These parts, if not clearly differentiated from one another and separated out from each other, overlap and bring about major problems in our feelings, our enjoyment, and our functioning. But now we must define more clearly the third figure in the Separation Triangle. This figure is that of the Individual.

Who is the Individual? The Individual is you, the person who is reading this book, and who is saying, "I am going to do this, and this is how I am going to do it. I am going to read the book and follow the steps and see exactly what I must do." The Individual is the *whole you* who is concerned with creating for himself a more satisfying life.

In Separation Therapy, the Individual plays special and very specific roles:

SETTING UP AND MAINTAINING THE SEPARATION

It is the Individual who performs the act of the imagination which separates the Child and the Adult out of himself and places each at the distance of five feet.

It is the Individual's major function to maintain this separation of the Child and the Adult at all times during the practice of the technique, especially at the beginning. This separation, or separateness, is what will allow each to develop properly in his respective role.

MANAGING THE DIALOGUE

It is by means of the dialogue that this development actually takes place, and the management of the dialogue becomes the responsibility of the Individual.

The Individual initiates the dialogues between the Adult and the Child; that is, he decides that a dialogue is indicated. He also is the medium, the voice through which the Child and the Adult express themselves, though he does not enter the actual discussion except *as* a voice.

KEEPING THE CHILD AND THE ADULT IN THEIR SEPARATE ROLES

Once the dialogue is begun, the Individual uses all his attention to remain watchful. What he is watching for is that the Adult figure and the Child figure *always* remain in their respective roles: the Child always a child, the Adult striving to be strong, capable, and protective. At no time must the two exchange roles, for then the dialogue becomes unproductive. The Individual must establish the characters of the two figures; then he steps back and lets them improvise and be spontaneous within the strictly defined roles that have been set for them.

Let us translate this into a simple example of how you, as the Individual, manage a dialogue keeping the two figures separate. You wake up at seven o'clock one morning feeling terrible and depressed. You, the Individual—your total experience of yourself—decide that you had better have a dialogue to figure out what is going on and what to do about it. You realize you must leave for work in an hour and it will take you a half hour to attend to your bathroom needs and have breakfast. So you decide you have another half hour for a dialogue. You decide the time will be now, at seven. You go into another room so you can have the dialogue aloud without awakening your spouse. The following is an example of a possible dialogue between Little and Big:

Dialogue #19

LITTLE: I feel sad, Big. I feel like crying.

BIG: Tell me what is troubling you. I will help you.

LITTLE: I think you made a mistake on your report yesterday, and I am afraid the boss will be angry with you and that frightens me.

BIG: I understand how you feel. Don't be frightened. If my boss becomes angry with me, I will handle it, and I will take care of you no matter what happens. I haven't made a mistake for months, and I'm entitled to make one once in a while without being put down too severely. Besides my boss is nice and understanding. Anyway, this is not your problem. It is mine. Don't worry about it. I will make sure that he doesn't hurt you.

LITTLE: I feel better. I am not sad anymore.

In this brief dialogue, each has remained in his proper role. However, if the dialogue should start badly and one or both roles become confused, or one or the other act improperly, it is the Individual's responsibility to be watchful and to stop if he feels it becoming unprofitable:

Dialogue #20

LITTLE: I feel sad, Big. I feel like crying.

BIG: I don't feel good either.

LITTLE: You never help me. You complain more than I do. What good are you to me anyway?

BIG: You're just a pain in the neck. I have enough troubles without dealing with you.

LITTLE: You're a miserable bastard. I'll never trust you again.

BIG: That suits me fine. You're nothing but a nuisance anyway.

Big is acting not like an adult but rather like an angry sibling. This is an example of an incorrect and unproductive dialogue, of which there may be many when the technique first begins. You, the Individual, realizing that it is incorrect, can terminate it and begin again either then or later.

STRENGTHENING THE ADULT

In addition, the Individual has another special and very vital role: It is the Individual who gives support and encouragement to the Adult figure. Many times in the dialogue—and in the real world—the wobbly and uncertain Adult figure will not yet be strong enough to know what to say and do, and it is the Individual who has to bolster and strengthen him and help him to grow. The Individual will say things to the adult like, "You are smarter than you know. You may not like what is happening, but you will be able to cope with it."

The Adult accepts what the Individual tells him because the Individual is telling him what he wants to hear, and although he may not accept it immediately, with frequent repetition, and by hearing it over and over again, the Adult reaches the stage at which he really believes what he hears and can act on it. And, as the Adult performs more and more effectively, controls the Child, and manages the Child's destructive behavior, he becomes stronger and more mature.

The Individual is what we think of as the total experience of ourselves—the self that we know.

Separation Therapy takes the component parts of this Individual and separates them out so that the Child can be helped to be a happy, nondestructive child and the Adult can be helped to become strong and mature.

6

The Separation Triangle: Technical Steps in Separating

We are now ready to describe the process of the complete and accurate separation of the Child and the Adult out of the Individual —the technical steps in the separation. This description will furnish the reader with the basic tool he needs to begin his own separation in earnest, and these steps can be referred to as many times as necessary as he progresses through the book. Also, the reader has the benefit of the group's experience, so he can begin using the full technique at once, just as it is presented here. It might seem from the previous discussion that practicing the specific steps would not be important. Be assured they are most important. For the person who wishes to derive real and lasting benefit from the technique, this procedure is absolutely essential. It is not enough to think, "Oh, I don't need to bother with that part—I can do well enough without it." This may be so if you know your childhood was a nurturing one, and your Child and Adult are in harmony. You are one of the fortunate people for whom only a superficial knowledge of the concept may work to solve a problem for you.

For most people, however, a firm and complete separation is the basis for success with the technique. Separating and staying separate are so essential, as we have repeated so often, because the Adult is freed of the troublesome Child so the Adult can mature. The nature of most people's problems has to do with the Child and the Adult being so enmeshed that the individual cannot distinguish one from the other. He thinks of his strong Adult as his "I" ("I can play a good game of bridge"), and the troublesome Child when he is acting up he also thinks of as "I" ("I'm stupid. I'm always making mistakes"). He is not aware that these need to be regarded as two separate entities.

Since most people are so confused about these two parts, it is especially important to establish and maintain a clear and definite separation, so the Adult can function unencumbered. It is not easy to unmesh the parts of the personality, but it is important to do so in order to be objective about them and to work on them. Thus a precise series of steps can be most helpful.

At this point, then, the authors will take the reader step by step through the specific acts of the imagination required in separating —splitting the Child and the Adult—which lead up to the dialogue.

1. Visualize the child that you were as clearly as possible, at any age up to five or six. It might be of help to use a photograph of yourself at that age to help make the visualization more concrete.

2. Give the child a childhood name that you were called, an endearment (Tina honey) or a nickname (Bunny) or a diminutive (Willie), or whatever name you yourself wish to call this child.

3. Imagine this child at any age up to five, sometimes as an infant, sometimes older, but never much older than five. But imagine him always with the ability to talk and to be understood at any age, even infancy.

4. Imagine this child with all of the characteristics of the child you actually were at any period up to age five. If you can't remember, conjecture, and you will probably be right. Or take an honest look into your present feelings. If you are having problems, these feelings will probably be the same as the feelings you had when you were a child. If you were a lonely child, your Child is still lonely; if you were anxious, he is still anxious; if you felt unloved, so does this Child; if you were sullen or hostile, or frightened, so is this Child. Imagine him as the source of all your unreasoning emotions, all your anger, depression, fear, feelings of inadequacy, and as the source of all the feelings and behaviors which work against your best interests. But also be aware that he is the source as well of all your joyfulness, playfulness, and capacity for enjoying life. In addition, realize that this Child is no more intelligent than you were up to age five. He cannot solve your adult problems, and he will never be able to solve them. He sees and interprets things as they seem to be to his childish mind. He remains ever a child, and he remains ever in need of reassurance, nonjudgmental acceptance, the unreserved love one would give to a cherished child, and limits—the loving discipline all children want and need.

5. Visualize the Adult, seeing him as you know the adult part of you to be when you are at your best; sensible, calm, capable, with your own special strengths in particular areas. Visualize your adult especially in the role of "good-enough mother." All of this describes Big You.

These were the preparations. Now for the actual separation:

6. The separation takes place when you, the Individual, visualize both the Child, Little, and the Adult, Big, as split out of your body, so that each can stand alone and apart. Big and Little should be imagined as at least five or six feet from each other.

7. Place the Adult, Big, on your stronger side and the Child, Little, on the weaker side. (Right-handedness makes the right side stronger and the left side weaker.)

8. You, the Individual, remain in the center as an objective observer, and as the voice who speaks for each part. Big and Little then carry on a dialogue through you, the Individual, who speaks for each of them, just as in role playing.

9. When you speak for Little, your body must take on the mannerisms and speech of a child. You must be that child. If Little is on your left side, you look up and across to your right as Little speaks to Big, whom you visualize as actually standing there. In taking the role of Big and speaking for him, look to the left and down as Big speaks to Little, actually visualizing the Child in whatever mood or posture he may be in at the time Big is talking to him. In the role of Big, you take on the body language of an erect, strong, sensible, responsible adult, whose main function is to help the Child when the Child is troubled, as he so often is.

10. Let us repeat that it is the function of the Individual to maintain the separation *of the Child and the Adult. As a kind of mediator, the Individual is in a position to observe both the Child and the Adult in action. He watches to see that the Child always behaves like a Child, and that the Adult always acts and thinks as an Adult—and that the two never exchange roles.*

What we have outlined may seem puzzling, but the reader should not let that stop him. As we have said, it is not necessary for the beginner to fully understand this technique. The important thing is to begin it the best way he can, and it will start to work.

You are now ready to start the dialogue, but it is at this point that most of the resistance takes place. It is necessary, therefore, to discuss resistances more fully in order to help the reader over this hurdle.

Resistance

In dealing with the resistances when starting to use this method, we must first enumerate some of the rationalizations that may be used to convince yourself not to start. Of course, you can toss the whole thing off as being a lot of foolishness. But if you get past this stage, you may tell yourself that the Child in you is quite happy and well taken care of and the Adult is doing well too. If this is really the case, when you begin the dialogue you will find this out and no harm will be done. But many will not even be able to fool themselves on this score. What you will probably find instead is a feeling of embarrassment.

There is, of course, a certain awkwardness in talking to oneself. But the real resistance here is almost always the reluctance to admit the existence of the Child in you. There is usually so much shame about this admission that the Child is totally denied. We have become so used to keeping this Child hidden in the closet. There have been so many admonitions, like "Act your age," "Stop babying yourself," "Don't be such a crybaby," "Stop acting like such a weakling," "You ought to be ashamed of yourself for crying," "You're such a child," "You're always begging," "Be a man," that they have sunk deep into our self-esteem system.

But the *shame* about being a baby is only a small part of the difficulty. When we acknowledge the presence of the Child, we also admit that there is a part of us that is very needy. And when we admit our need, we become very vulnerable. This makes us extremely frightened. Once we know we need people to love us and to accept us and we remove our shield about it, we can be very severely hurt if this approval is not forthcoming. Our shield protects us from feeling hurt. Many of us, because of negative experiences in our childhood, may feel that the Child in us, the real core of us, is unacceptable. Reactions from people around us have given us this negative reflection of ourselves. When we now let the Child out, we feel quite certain that these responses will be repeated and that we will only re-experience the original pain. We are so certain that the response will be negative that we cannot even trust the Adult part of ourselves to be kind and loving and accepting of the Child.

And then to compound the problem, aside from the hurt, negative responses will also make the Child angry. We may be frightened that this primitive anger from childhood, if unleashed, will destroy others as well as ourselves. We may also be fearful of retaliation for this anger.

But we have to remember that none of these things can or will actually happen, because the dialogues can be modified or stopped at any time.

In beginning the practice of the technique through the dialogues, we have to be tolerant of our resistances, understand them, and not give in to them. We must simply make a decision to give this method a try. For once the starting barrier is broken, success will spur us on to continue working at it. But even here we must be aware of a strong tendency to resist and stop the process.

The degree of resistance varies with different people. For some, resistance can be very strong. The more resistance there is, the harder it will be to begin or to sustain Separation Therapy. Some of the standard resistances are these:

I feel foolish doing it.
I'm afraid that if I get into this maybe I won't be able to stop carrying on the dialogue. Then I'll be crazy—a split personality.
I hate the Little Girl and I can't see her clearly.
I can say the words but don't seem to be in touch with the feelings.
I'm afraid I'm opening up a hornet's nest and I'm scared to start.

It takes too much discipline and needs too much work in order not to give up. I have always taken the easy way, and now Little and Big must continue to carry on the dialogue at all times. This I find hard to sustain.

I have resistance to everything. But this time the resistance is much greater. First I resist, then I develop guilt feelings, and when I'm guilty enough I operate well.

I couldn't do it. I couldn't separate. It was very difficult. I felt I couldn't do it. It seems to be an "asking" situation on the part of the Adult, not a telling one. I had a problem in keeping separate. I was waiting for Little to give me advice. I get a headache as I talk to the Little Girl because, as I give her love, I realize how deprived I was.

I am self-conscious about it, but it is more than that. By doing this, talking to the Child once, it will be a permanent kind of change that I don't want. I'm not ready to separate from the Child.

There is something irrevocable about it. I'm uncomfortable talking about it. I don't want to do it and I am enjoying the resistance. If I give in I will lose something. It is connected with masochism. If I give up hurt, I will be losing something. . . . Besides, everyone is doing it and I am not special anymore.

I don't see the Little Girl, and what I can't see I don't like.

I'm skeptical. I don't believe in it. I can't see the Little Boy and I don't want anything experimental at this point.

It seems ridiculous to me. It's a waste of time and I don't have time. It's as if I'm not permitted to be happy. My Little Girl is unhappy.

These are some of the typical comments people have made in putting off starting the process of Separation Therapy. You will undoubtedly come up with some of these or some like these too. About resistance, try to see it as an expected phenomenon rather than as an insuperable hurdle. That in itself will help. You are not the exception if you resist at first. Quite the contrary. Both authors themselves exhibited a great deal of resistance to starting their own dialogues, even when they were uniformly enthusiastic about the method for other people. But once they started it themselves, it worked. Remember, at first it may seem silly and awkward and mechanical. You will say the words without feeling the emotion behind them. Don't allow this to discourage you. Keep at it. If you don't feel loving toward the Child, keep playing it as a role. "Act and you will become." There is enough validity in the formulation and the technique so that with a certain degree of will, most are able to overcome the initial resistance and begin almost at once to benefit from this technique.

CASE HISTORY

Virginia

Virginia, who was emotionally and physically immobilized a good part of her life, expressed a desire to remain anonymous because of the possibility of a professional career. However, the authors would like to include her case history and some of her dialogues. Through our Separation Therapy, she was able to regress to her very early childhood and experience the emotions she probably felt as an infant, although most people do not go back this far.

Virginia's parents were killed in an automobile accident when she was about a year old. It appears from her dialogues that she has spent much of her life longing and searching for her mother.

In October 1973, in the group, when the seed of Separation Therapy began to take root and to crystallize into a concrete technique, Virginia began to show dramatic results. She worked on the Separation Therapy technique for several months without success until she was convinced that there was just no Little Girl there. But she did not give up, and tried to get in touch with her every day, until one day Little just popped out and began to unleash a torrent of words and emotions. Little talked incessantly for months. Hers were continuing, spontaneous monologues—not dialogues—in which Virginia felt that Little unleashed the core problem that might never have revealed itself, and that might have given her trouble for the rest of her life. The basic problem to which she constantly returned was always the same. "I want my mommy, where is she, and why did they take her away from me? Why did she leave me?" Virginia said that, as many of Little's feelings of abandonment began to pour out, she found herself crying constantly with Little. This experience was most disconcerting, especially when Little originally broke through.

Virginia worked on the Separation Therapy technique for many months. During this time she wrote dialogues almost daily. As the dialogues continued, and as Big separated more and more from Little, she sent the following letter to her therapist:

101

I wonder if you are aware of the fact that you have discovered something very marvelous and very helpful. In fact, it seems to me that you have made a great breakthrough in the field of psychiatry and psychotherapy.

I have been in therapy with you for a long time, twelve years to be exact. I know that to someone who has never been in therapy twelve years may seem so long, but it really is not, especially when we realize that problems start from the day we are born, or maybe earlier.

The marvelous part of discovering the Little Girl in myself and separating her out is that, through this technique, I discovered what happened to me as far back as infancy. At the time I entered therapy, I had so many problems that it is amazing to me now that I was functioning at all. The most obvious problem to me was that I was *so slow and repressed.* I felt practically nothing. You helped me through so much, and then something very important happened. It was what might be called a missing link. One day this winter you told us about the Little Child, in each of us, that had to be separated out. At first it just seemed to be another helpful principle like positive suggestion, which is helpful up to a point. Then, however, the whole group really got into it. It was just amazing that we discovered things and feelings that we never knew were there. I would like to tell you briefly some of the things that happened to me. If one person is helped by my experience, the Separation Therapy technique will prove rewarding.

My therapy, as I saw it then, revolved around events that happened from approximately three and a half years of age. But now I know that *my problems started when I was an infant.* I can see now that my fears and phobias started when I was nine months old or even earlier. At that time my parents were killed in an accident. Through this technique I have been able to go back to infancy. The original trauma was a separation from my mother. That is why this Little Girl has been looking for her mommy all her life. *By my discovering this Little Girl, separating her out and talking to her, she has told me all I need to know. This was the missing link that I had been searching for so long.* This Little Girl told me exactly how she felt as an infant, how much she was loved by her grandparents, with whom she lived after the death of her parents, and how much she meant to them. She told me all about her grandma and grandpa. She told me about the catastrophic trauma of separation from the mother. I can see now that this is the missing link.

As opposed to conventional therapy, the Separation Therapy for me has been moving very fast. *It is a direct route to the unconscious.* In a matter of a few months I have discovered things that I didn't know after twelve years of therapy. I believe it will really revolutionize psychotherapy.

Virginia/Dialogue #21

In this dialogue, Virginia's Little is taking her back to the first year of her life.

BIG: How are you tonight, Little?

LITTLE: I am sort of fine, Big. Today you took me to a party. There were nice cakes and candy there. Well, Big, you were talking to all the ladies, and there were lots of children there. I wanted to play with all those children *but I couldn't get out, BIG.* You know, I love houses with yards and grass and parties in the backyard. There was a gigantic tree right in the middle of that yard, at my mommy's house, when I was little. It was a pretty house with a pretty yard. When I was a baby she used to put me to sleep under that tree, and when I woke up I saw the branches moving.

Well, one day when I was just an itty-bitty baby, my mommy had a party in the yard. Someone was holding me but I don't know who—maybe it was Grandpa. You know, once I had a grandpa, and a grandmother too. I wonder where they went? Do you think they are in heaven watching me, Big? Well anyway, Mommy wore a white dress. She was beautiful. She had blond hair and she wore a white dress, and there were cakes and drinks, but I only got a bottle, Big. I wonder why? Grandpa was nice. He had black hair and he was a little fat, but not too much. I would like to see that house again. Please take me there. You could do it—I know you can. I have to go back there.

Please, please take me there, Big. I have to go back to Mommy.

Virginia/Monologue #22

Little talks almost constantly.

LITTLE: You know, Big, I love my grandma and grandpa very much, but
not as much as Mommy. I keep Grandma up all night with my
crying. You know why I cry? I cry for my mommy. I cry all night,
but she doesn't come. I know she loves me. She knows everything,
Mommy. But why doesn't she come to take me home? I am so
tired of crying. If Mommy came and took me home, I would never
cry again, Big. Where is my mommy? Why doesn't she hurry and
come for me? Grandpa brought me a teddy bear. It was brown and
white, and Mommy put it in my playpen for me. Do you know I
wouldn't go anywhere without my teddy bear? Where is my teddy
bear now, Big? I miss my teddy bear. He needs me to take care
of him. He is so lonesome. Why, all he does is cry all the time.
Poor little bear, you are so unhappy. Big, I have to go back—you
have to take me back. Mommy is looking for me. She is frantic.
She is in a panic. What will she do without me? I am her little
baby, and she needs me. I miss the trees in the yard, too. I love
that tree, Big. I miss the grass, too. Where is Mommy? When will
Mommy come? Please tell her to hurry. I can't wait any longer.
I am so tired of crying. But I have to cry every night so Mommy
will come for me. Please tell her to hurry. Please, please, please.

Virginia/Monologue #23

This is not a dialogue, but Virginia is still recapturing very early
childhood feelings.

LITTLE: I am four years old, Big. I am happy today. We are going to the
country. I am riding in a car with my grandma and grandpa.
Someone is driving the car, but I don't know who. Maybe it is
Uncle Donald, Big. Ahead of the car I see mountains. We go up
the hill, and I think this time we will get to the top, but we never
do. There is always another mountain in front of us. Funny, isn't
it, Big? We are riding in a black car; that is why I am so happy.
You know, this car is the same as my daddy's car. Maybe it is his

car. Big, I bet he sent his car to bring Mommy back. My mommy lives in the country. I bet I am going home to her. That's why I am so excited and happy today.

Little is still longing for her mommy, and hoping to get back to her.

Virginia/Monologue #24

Most of the following is the child talking, but she is still revealing early infancy feelings. This is evidently before the first year, when her mother was killed.

LITTLE: You know, Big, I have a secret to tell you. Do you want to know what it is? I love Grandpa. He came over to my house with a teddy bear. I love that teddy bear. I have to have it near me all the time, or I cry. I am crying now, Big. Where's my teddy bear? I have to find it. Who will take care of it when it cries, if I don't have it? If I find my teddy bear I can find Mommy. Where is she? Why can't I find her? I can't stop crying until Mommy comes. Mommy isn't here, Big, but Grandma and Grandpa are here. They are watching me tonight. I love Grandpa, Big. I have Grandpa and my teddy bear. Grandma brings in bottle . . . I take bottle. I wake up. Maybe Mommy is back.

Virginia/Dialogue #25

LITTLE: It is thundering, Big. It frightens me. I am in the carriage under the tree. Mommy picks me up fast. Then she runs into the house with me. Big, would you make a bargain with me?
BIG: What kind of a bargain would you like to make, Little?
LITTLE: Well, Big, please don't say I am silly.
BIG: I never say you are silly, Little. I love you.
LITTLE: Well, here is the bargain. I know you want to work. Well, I will let you work if you will help me find my mommy.

Virginia/Dialogue #26

There is more separation indicated in the following. Big, separating from Little, is assuming responsibility for Little. She is even putting limits on her, which is very important.

BIG: What's the matter, Little?

LITTLE: I want my mommy . . . yes, I do. That's why I am so bad. But I can never find her again. She is gone forever, and that's why I am so sad.

BIG: Well, it's true that she is gone, but the love she gave you will be a part of you forever.

LITTLE: I guess you are right. I will try to be better for you from now on. I really do love you.

BIG: I love you too—very much. You are such a good, sweet little girl and I will always take care of you. You can play and sing and dance and look at the trees. I know you love trees and grass.

LITTLE: I do love grass and trees. I love the country. You see, Mommy and Daddy and I lived in a beautiful house in the country. It was summertime, and we were outside on the grass all summer. I was so happy there. I wish I could be there again. I can never see my mommy again.

BIG: I know it's hard for a little girl to accept that, but I will be your mommy now and you never have to be afraid again. I will always take care of you.

LITTLE: But I want Mommy. I know you are my mommy and I love you, but I want her.

BIG: Well, there are some things in life we can't have, but we can have other things. [Virginia is putting limits on Little.]

LITTLE: But I am just a little girl, and I want what I want.

Virginia/Dialogue #27

During many months of writing dialogues, Little continued to express feelings involving the first nine months of her life. Virginia said that when the early feelings of loneliness began to burst forth, she found herself crying constantly.

LITTLE: Hello, Big. I am an itty-bitty baby. Daddy is in the car. Mommy is in the car. I am in the car. Mommy is holding me in her arms. She gives me bottle. I fall asleep. Wake up in Grandma's house. Grandpa's there. Aunt Audrey there too. Other man there too. Everyone at table. Where's my teddy bear, Big? Where's my grandpa, Big? Where are they? I love Grandpa. I miss him. Take me to Grandpa—please, please. Please, please take me to my Grandpa. I always cry, Big. All I do is cry. Do you know why I cry? I cry because I can't find my mommy. I am in the carriage, Big. I cry—Mommy comes. She picks me up. Why doesn't she come for me now when I cry? What will I do? Where is Mommy, Big? I cry all the time, but I still can't find Mommy. What will I do? I don't know what to do. I must have my mommy, BIG.

BIG: Little, I will be your mommy now, and I will always take care of you and protect you. Isn't that enough, Little?

[Therapist's comment: Big is assuming the responsibility for protecting and taking care of Little. In this process, Big is strengthening her adult.]

Virginia/Dialogue #28

In this dialogue Big and Little are separated.

BIG: Little, please tell me something. Do you want to go to New York tomorrow?

LITTLE: I don't think so.

BIG: Why not?

LITTLE: Well, I get nervous when I'm in the city. I'm afraid I'll get lost.

BIG: Why do you get nervous, Little?

LITTLE: Well, it's because I'm so angry.

BIG: Why are you so angry, Little?

LITTLE: *Because I tried to talk to you for so long and you just wouldn't listen. So I gave you a lot of fears and phobias. I couldn't help it. I just had to get even. On the outside I was always good, because I had to be a nice little girl like you. But I have a lot of fight in me, Big. You never knew it, but I have guts and I am very spirited —not like you at all. But now you want to see me full of life. I don't want to separate from you. Well, I don't mind, but in a way I like* to be close to you. But you know what? If I still can see you and talk to you, we can be two different people. I will be Little and you will be my mommy, my Big. I never wanted to grow up anyway. It's so much fun being a little girl. I can do all the fun things, and maybe I can help you have fun. Please let me help you, because I love you. I really do.

BIG: I love you so much too. And you can help me very much by being a happy little girl.

LITTLE: You make me feel happy.

Virginia/Dialogue #29

LITTLE: You know, Big, we are all in the living room. I am in my playpen on a green blanket on the floor. Daddy is here and Mommy is here, and Aunt Audrey and her boyfriend. Mommy said Aunt Audrey is going to marry him. He is nice. Grandpa is here, and Grandma too. Mommy said she is so happy for Audrey. I remember the kitchen in my mommy's house. It was very long and there was something in the middle. There was a dining room too, with a gigantic table and lots of chairs. From the dining room you could go into the living room. Where is my crib, Big? I can't find it. I am lost. I don't know, Big, I love you very much, but I want Mommy. Please take me to her.

BIG: I don't know where to find her.

LITTLE: You could find her if you wanted to. Just please try for me, Big.

BIG: We'll see. Maybe.

LITTLE: Don't say maybe. I need my mommy. What will I do without her, Big? I need her. I want her. Please, Big. Where did she go? I miss her. I love her. My mommy went away. I am so confused, Big. Everyone says I am such a good little girl, and I am precious. Please tell me why.

BIG: Why, you are an angel. But sometimes unfortunate things happen in life, and even grown-ups can't do much about it. We just have to take it. [Big is helping Little take frustration.]

LITTLE: *I will never love anyone again. Why should I? I won't laugh or sing or play or run anymore. I will just be sad.*

Virginia/Dialogue #30

Virginia, who has always felt unloved and rejected, discovered, through this technique and the dialogue exercises connected with it, that she had been very much loved by many people during her early life. Had it not been for the Separation technique, she might have gone through life totally unaware of the love that had been truly hers. But here she is still talking about the first nine months of her life.

BIG: How are you, Little Virginia?

LITTLE: Not too good. I loused you up again. I took over and didn't let you go to the audition. I am terrible.

BIG: I don't think you are terrible. You are just an unhappy little girl.

LITTLE: Did you know that my mommy went away and left me? That is why I am so sad and unhappy. I remember I was very little then —too little to walk. Why, I was just starting to stand. My mommy and daddy lived in a big house. There were so many rooms. It was in the country and there were lots of trees outside. We had a maid to do all the housework, and Mommy would spend all day playing with me and kissing me. I had a nice daddy, too. A lot of other people were around too. They came and went, and everyone liked me. I don't remember what happened. *But one day my mommy wasn't there anymore.*

Virginia/Monologue #31

LITTLE: I'm thinking of leaving, Big. I just have to have Mommy and you won't take me, so I think I will go myself. Of course I won't stay overnight, not unless you come with me. But I don't see you taking me to Mommy. What if I go in the morning and come back at night? That way, Big, you can work because that is what you want and need, and you won't have to worry about me all day. You see, Mommy will take care of me. She misses me so, Big. You see, Big, Mommy is Mommy. Mommy is my mommy, and I miss her so much, but I'm glad you know what's bothering me now because I feel a little better now. At least I can say "Mommy" without crying.

Virginia/Dialogue #32

This is a separated dialogue, in which Little is beginning to accept Virginia as a loving mother.

BIG: Hello, Little. How are you today?

LITTLE: I am very fine—really I am, Big.

BIG: How did you like your vacation?

LITTLE: I loved it. I really did. You know, I love riding in the car and I saw so many things. I had a good time.

BIG: Did you get nervous at all on your vacation?

LITTLE: Yes, I got panicky.

BIG: When did you get panicky, Little?

LITTLE: Well, the first time I got panicky we were almost in the country and it was like the wilderness. There was nothing around. A little girl could die out there and no one would ever know. I was scared to death, Big.

BIG: You know I will always take care of you. So you don't ever have to worry, Little.

LITTLE: I know that, but sometimes I get scared.

BIG: Well, you don't have to worry anymore. I am always with you. I will do all the worrying and you just have all the fun.

LITTLE: O.K. I feel better about it now. You know, Big, I love you. You're smart. You are wonderful. You are so smart; you're as smart as my mommy. You want to know a secret, Big?

BIG: Yes, I would love to know a secret.

LITTLE: Well, I will tell you. *You know, now that I have you I can get along without my mommy.* You know I still would love to have my mommy. *But now that you are my mommy I can manage without her.*

BIG: Why, I think that's wonderful. I am very happy and proud of you, Little. You are a very good little girl.

LITTLE: I am going to throw you a kiss, Big.

For some reason Virginia was able to probe into her early childhood feelings, and was able to get in touch with a deep-rooted feeling of abandonment.

She stayed with her childhood feelings longer than any of the others in the group. As she separated from Little and assumed responsibility for her, and as Little learned to love and trust Big and accept her as her mother, Virginia was free to take charge of her own life. She is continuing to make progress.

CASE HISTORY

Sam

Sam, father of two young children, David and Susan (eight and four at the time), came into treatment at the suggestion of his wife, who said that she could no longer live under the conditions that existed in their home. Sam was not aware that there was anything wrong with the way they were living, but the family lived in constant fear of his homecoming because of his unpredictable and terrorizing conduct.

Sam was withdrawn and antisocial. He was completely out of touch with his feelings except when his anger surged up and overwhelmed him.

Sam was brought up extremely deprived. His mother and father fought constantly, and his mother told him how much she disliked his father, an honest, hardworking laborer who always provided well for his family. She overprotected Sam, and at the same time reduced him by laughing at his mistakes and telling him that he would never amount to anything much. But she also told him that he would never have to worry because she would always take care of him. Sam grew up hating his father, and honestly believing he would never have to take care of himself—his mother would always be there to provide for him. His father, infuriated by his wife, by her treatment of Sam, and by her rejection of him, often threatened to leave the house, adding angrily that they would both starve because neither of them could earn a living. This frightened Sam and made him insecure. It appears that his mother never allowed a good relationship to develop between father and son.

When Sam first came into therapy many years ago, he was operating on a most immature level, very dependent, withdrawn, and emotionally flat. It was impossible for him to operate in any area as an adult. He had problems working, playing, and studying. He was unable to concentrate on what he was doing and to stay with it for any length of time. "I was so removed from myself that I was like a mechanical robot that was being operated and manipulated."

113

He was unable to relate to anyone, including his wife and children. He was extremely antagonistic toward his father and very much attached to his mother, but described her as a cruel, domineering, belittling, destructive woman.

Sam began therapy at a very low level. He was attached to his daughter, though he was rejecting of her. He was hostile toward his son, with whom he was in competition. He was extremely rejecting of his wife, from whom he wanted constant nurturing.

Sam's wife is a bright, capable, warm, outgoing woman. She too has great feelings of rejection and is full of guilt. She, a masochist, took a lot of punishment, which she quickly suppressed and converted into physical illness. The children, though bright, operated on an inefficient and self-sabotaging level for many years. They seemed to lack motivation for success and even seemed to gravitate toward failure.

As his therapy evolved, Sam began to realize that he was extremely hostile toward authority. "I misinterpret people's motives and become angry in advance." He was a very frightened person—afraid of death, afraid of living, afraid of rejection, and afraid of work. He expressed a lot of hatred toward his parents for making him feel that he would never be able to support himself.

Over a period of years in therapy Sam continued to make progress slowly. At times it appeared that he was developing insight and seemed better able to handle his reality. *And though he expressed a great need to change, he would at constantly recurring intervals regress to being the little boy who was unable to function. All his years in therapy were up and down, and though he managed better more often and for longer periods of time, he regressed when a situation involved his childlike emotions.* He constantly built up anger and hostility in himself. "No matter where I turned I was building up hostilities . . . and I released these hostilities wherever and whenever I could—mostly on my wife and children. My bosses were also punished by me in the most childish and immature way. I did things wrong just to punish them for not giving me what I wanted when I wanted it. I was hostile all the time. It is almost unbelievable to think that I was so low and so sick without ever having any awareness of it for the first seven years of my therapy." But with the insights he was gaining in therapy, Sam found that he was better able to relate to his daughter and son, and to give of himself up to a certain point when they needed his help. "When people ask too much of me I still reject them—I still am not able to give. But I see it, and I see it at work and find that I am better able to control it." *Sam still had problems working efficiently and following through at work.* "I find that I want to avoid reality, as I have always done when problems arise. Though I am doing better, I still want from my daughter the kind of approval and acceptance and love that I didn't get as a teenager, and I want from my wife the tender loving I never got from my mother. But I know that I must get down to the hard facts of what I have to do for others, not what I want them to do for me."

Sam released terrific hostilities toward his therapist, who he felt was being too hard on him. As he communicated these feelings to her, he was better able to communicate with his family, who at this point were beginning to fight him when he tried to browbeat them. Though his son turned to him and for the first time said, "You give me a pain in the neck," Sam accepted this anger because he felt his son was justified. The following day he congratulated him for having the courage to give his honest feelings. This showed progress and more control than he had previously had.

For the past five years, Sam's relationship with his father, who was dying, had become warm and loving. Of him he said, "I feel that he has left me something that I can build on. I took a lot of strength from my father, who I realize now had a lot of strength to give. For some time we've been closer than ever, and I cherish the relationship. He wanted to give me a sense of responsibility as I was growing up, and to teach me to stand on my own two feet and to work. I resented this because I was overprotected by my mother and I wasn't capable of doing what he wanted of me."

Though Sam became stronger in some areas and for longer periods of time, he still had many problems involving work—fear of finding a new job and insecurities surrounding it. He still had problems with his son when he (Sam) regressed. He felt stupid because of his lack of formal schooling, which he talked about overcoming by going back to school. Sam had always blamed everyone else for his mistakes. He began to understand that it was frequently he who was at fault. There was a difference in the way he was beginning to think, but he was still up and down a good part of the time. When his daughter came home from her honeymoon, Sam had a violent reaction, and understood that his attachment to her was deeper than he had realized.

Over the years, as he developed more insight into the reasons for the way he functioned, he was able to get better jobs with more responsibility, involving traveling around the country. He was very frightened with each new responsibility, and though he continued to regress and get out of touch with reality at times, he was still able to function on a more mature level. He was becoming more aware of, and getting more in touch with, his symptoms. He could feel when he withdrew, by a fuzziness in the head, by clogged ears, and by his inability to hear or see what was going on. He said of himself, "When I was a child, I was withdrawn. Now I know the difference between fantasy and reality. I live between both. This is the kind of inner strength that can give birth to real adult progress. Now it remains for me to set my sights and work in those directions." It appeared as if he was making a decision to stay in touch with reality.

The therapy group he was in helped. The interplay among the other people in the group proved most valuable. "I can see that my son is taking from me the things he needs: strength, love, and understanding. When I am able to stay with it, my actions are mature. My son, a college dropout, who had been going through a hostile, traumatic adolescence, is beginning to show remarkable changes. There seems to be a real change for the better in both of us, especially since I am becoming more aware of my hostility." Sam was beginning to be less angry for longer periods of time. He was relating better to his wife as a husband, and to his daughter as a father. Though he was doing well in many areas, at times he still continued to have problems on the job. "Though things are working out a little better, I haven't been thinking, planning, and working efficiently. I've neglected important follow-up calls because they were complaints and I couldn't face them. I have loused up jobs involving big, important firms, and I am scared of being exposed and losing my job."

He continued to talk more freely about his jealousies, his sex drives, and what he considered abnormal fantasies which involved an easy life with someone to take care of him.

Over a period of years Sam continued to make progress except

116

when he permitted the Little Child within him to take over. Then his judgment was bad and he was no longer able to function like an adult. His therapist used many kinds of therapy with him, to which he seemed to respond at the time. His progress was continuous but slow until he began working with the Separation Therapy technique. Now he says of himself, "For me the Separation Therapy technique is the answer to real self-understanding."

About nine months ago he attempted to use Separation Therapy but found it difficult. The Child was tightly bound within him and at first he could not see him as a separate entity. "The more I tried to get him out, the more he refused. Meanwhile I continued my old pattern of making mistakes. I was making mistakes of omission, so that I was able to kid myself into thinking that I was not doing a bad job. I got away with a lot, but I made some bad blunders and when I thought of the day of reckoning, I got sick and petrified. I again became insecure and afraid of being fired." At this point Little popped out and attacked Big with a lifetime of bottled-up anger. *The following monologue ensued:*

LITTLE: You always do this. You make me sick and you scare me. You never took care of me. You never talked to me. You never knew I was there. You never gave me one happy day. Every day was hell. You go away. You always leave me with the problems. You make the problems—and then I have to face them. I can't take care of big problems. I'm only a little boy. Why do you do that to me? You don't care. I'm so f——ing mad at you I hate you. I want to hurt you. I want to get even. And I'm going to hurt you more and more and more . . . the way you have always hurt me.

After several months of Little Sammy's *monologues,* which varied in form and intensity—at times with anger and at times with tears —the therapist suggested that Big start to use *dialogues* in an effort to limit Little's hostility, which seemed to be self-destructive after so long a time. It was time for Big to help Little, who was constantly in trouble. But Big was not yet able to do it.

In the following dialogue, the reader will note that *Big* at this point is crying out in a *childish* way for help. Since Big and Little are not yet separated, Big continues to operate like a child.

117

Sam/Dialogue #33

LITTLE: I'm scared. I'm scared all the time when I go to work with you. I'm afraid that you are not going to do your job. Why don't you do your job, stupid? I'm not going to do your job. I can't do it. I'm too little. You got to do everything for *me*. You gotta be *good* to me. You gotta be good to me and *love* me and *take care* of me, 'cause if you do I'll be your friend. I'll be good and I'll help you.

BIG: I got a problem, Little, and I don't know how we're going to work this out. But we have to, and you are going to have to help me, Little, like when I can't get that order. Then I want to creep under the bed and hide and just go back into my shell. I feel like s——t and I leave you holding the bag. I can't do that, and you are going to have to help me, Little. We gotta figure out how I am going to help myself. When I see that I am going to crawl under that bed, don't let me do it. I know when it is happening. I get these signs—my ears get clogged, I get that faraway feeling, and I know I am going off. Then there is nobody left. There's nobody left to fight the battle—nobody there to do the job. And when I am in trouble, Little, will you help me? Will you help me, Little, will you? When I start to lose ground you're gonna have to say to me, "Big, get in there and fight because you're smart. You can do it. And I will help you, Big. Just keep fighting. You're smart, you can do it. . . . Stay with it." And if you tell me that, I won't run away because I want to be good to you, Little. *I need you to help me.*

More recently, Big said, "Now that I am using the Separation technique, I understand that all of my fears were childish fears. I dreaded each day, all of my life. Every morning was awakening to a nightmare. I couldn't do things that I should do, and did the things that I shouldn't, childish things like just wasting time, and playing when I should have been working, fantasizing when I should have been thinking out real problems. These were the escapes. And as a result I got into terrible trouble. I was terrified every day that something I should have done would catch up with me, and that I would be found out. All of my life I had fear—fears that I couldn't take care of myself, fears of insecurity, and fears of losing my job. When I copped out I didn't feel, I didn't see, I didn't hear, and I didn't even know what was happening around me. I was out of reality. And I was in real trouble."

In the following dialogue, the reader will see that Big is only partially separated from the child. Though he is beginning to make progress, Big is still long-winded, defensive, and a weak adult.

Sam/Dialogue #34

BIG: What's the matter, Little? Do you have a problem?

LITTLE: I'm scared, Big. I am scared that you are not going to do your job —that you are going to do what you always do. You go up and down, and you go away from doing your job; and you make me scared and I don't like it. I want you to be strong. I want you to take care of me. I can't do your job. You have to do it.

BIG: O.K., Little. I know how you feel because I feel that way too. I'm scared myself. I have lots of problems on the job. I want to run away, but that doesn't mean that I am going to. I am going to face whatever I have to. I am stronger than I have ever been. I am going to take care of you, Little, like you want to be taken care of, and I can do it. You won't ever have to worry about me, and when I have problems I will solve them one way or another. No sweeping under the rug anymore. It sounds good, doesn't it? It sounds good to me. I will get better and better every day. You watch me. I like having you with me all the time. I love you, Little. You are really good for me. When you tell me how you feel, that helps me too. When you are frightened and you want me to help you, tell me right away and I will do it. I want to do it for you. You'll have lots of fun. I will be very successful and I will be great. I feel it, don't you?

Sam/Dialogue #35

In this dialogue, Big seems to be separating more, and is becoming a stronger adult.

LITTLE: I got a funny feeling in my chest—like I'm out of breath . . . like a nervous feeling. When you were talking to Mom, I got the feeling that she won't love me and won't leave me her money. I'm afraid she'll give it to Robert instead of me. That worries me, because I want her to take care of me. She promised that she would. She said that she would always take care of me. She wanted only me. She didn't even want Papa. I don't want her to love anybody else. I don't want her to give her money to anyone else. I want her to give all her money to me, and that's why I am nervous.

BIG: I know how you feel, Little. I don't want her to give her money away either. It would be very nice for me to have . . . and it would be very good for you, too.

LITTLE: How can you manage without the money? You need the money and she promised it to you.

BIG: That's true. It will be nice if she gives it to me, but if she doesn't I will be able to manage.

LITTLE: But who will help you?

BIG: I will help myself. I am strong and I can work, and I will earn plenty of money for you and me. So stop worrying, Little. I love you and I always will take care of you.

As time went on, Sam was actually able to visualize both Little and Big, separated and conversing with each other. Big could see that Little was often in trouble, and when Big came to Little's assistance, Little saw Big as a strong, loving, gentle, and accepting parent. And Big saw Little as a needy, frightened, angry child to whom he gave complete acceptance. They came to understand each other and no longer needed lengthy dialogues to reassure each other.

Sam/Dialogue #36

This is one of the later, less wordy, dialogues:

LITTLE: Big, tell me you love me.

BIG: I love you.

LITTLE: Big, tell me that you will take care of me.

BIG: I will take care of you.

LITTLE: Big, tell me that you won't let anybody hurt me.

BIG: I won't let anybody hurt you.

LITTLE: Tell me I'm a good boy, Big.

BIG: You are a good boy.

LITTLE: I feel so good when you tell me that you love me and that you will take care of me. Tell me again.

BIG: I love you very much and I will take care of you always.

Though Sam has come a long way, he still regresses and withdraws, but for very much shorter periods of time. He has developed enough insight and awareness to quickly get in touch with the problems that are causing him to act in a childish way. He feels that it is only through the use of our Separation Therapy technique that he can continue to function on an adult level. When we consider where he started, we have to admit that he has made real progress. There is every reason to believe that he will continue to grow as long as he is able to maintain a separation between the Child and the Adult . . . nurtured by loving communication between the two.

As recently as five months ago Sam made the following remarks:

My awareness of feelings which for me were nonexistent has given a new dimension to living. I am capable of both receiving and giving happy, loving, as well as angry, feelings. The happy and loving feelings are a new experience for me, and I almost feel like a child with a new toy, realizing how well new acquaintances are accepting me. And for the very first time I spontaneously respond with the same warm feelings. My angry feelings are handled maturely. I know when I am angry and I am able to confront the person with whom I'm angry, keeping the Adult in control. I usually think what I am going to say, rather than getting angry and turning it inward. I actually feel like an adult for the first time in my life. I feel like a person and that I am my correct age, fifty. This too is a new feeling, because I had previously thought of myself as being much younger, weaker, more vulnerable, less knowledgeable—and in need of comfort and support from others. Now I know that no matter what the circumstances, I will be able to manage, and I am not fearful of making mistakes. Perhaps what is most important—I know that I will be happy in the future and that I will be able to cope with anything. I can manage. I am an adult.

Sam has progressed to the vice-presidency of his company.

7

Staying in Control: The Power Struggle

By no means must we assume that the Child will now allow himself to be led docilely by the hand in a generous, loving treaty with the Adult. Quite the opposite: The Child will fight a terrible, bloody, ruthless struggle to stay where he is and, to whatever degree he is doing it, keep the Adult at his mercy. We are aware of this whenever we try consciously to change or overcome a habit of *any* kind—how much more difficult to search out and change this crafty, hidden Child. It is not that the Child hates the Adult; what the Child is doing is using the Adult as an instrument to punish himself and to act out all his childish demands, emotions, and needs.

As we know, the Child is filled with rage, outrage, fear, loneliness, self-hate, self-pity; when he is feeling neglected and unloved he can be the most vicious animal in the world. He can be totally irrational and lacking in any understanding. He can pout and have temper tantrums. He can feel sorry for himself and moan and groan in misery and despair. He can make the world a terrible place for himself and for everyone around him. He can be negative, sad, hostile, moody, insecure, jealous, afraid, stupid, withdrawn, flat. He is purely motivated by "Give me what I want, when I want it, and just *because* I want it, or I'll create a hell on earth!"

The energy of the unloved Child is extremely hostile, and these feelings, easily recognizable in ourselves and in others around us, are so strong that the Adult is overwhelmed by them and at the mercy of the Child. When these feelings take over, it is a signal that the Child is in control and is in a power struggle to overwhelm the Adult. But this the Adult must not permit; if we are to succeed, it is the Adult who must stay in control.

Staying Aware

We know the Child is in trouble and is sabotaging us every time we have these feelings. These feelings of "upsetness" or discomfort are a signal that the Child needs help, has taken over the functioning of the Adult and has drowned him out. These feelings should be a strong signal to the Individual to place the Adult—Big—back in control. This is the Individual's first task. He must train himself to respond quickly to these feelings, separate the Child and the Adult out of himself, and let the Adult find out from the Child what the problem is. The Individual must train himself to be alert for the particular signs that tell him when his Child is taking over. He may feel sleepy. His head may feel tight. His ears may get stopped up or start to ring. He may feel stupid, or afraid, or jealous, or wiped out; whichever way, the Individual becomes aware that something is wrong. He must achieve the split second of awareness, so that the instant any of these things happens he can avert the power struggle and place the Adult immediately in control. This may not be easy, but the Individual must fight until this split second of awareness becomes a familiar response.

What the Adult Needs from the Child

It might be asked, If the Child is so destructive, why don't we simply discard him, and let our Adult manage our lives sensibly and successfully? The answer is that we must not and we dare not, because it is the Child in us who is the most real and precious part of us—is

124

the *real* person—with all the taste for fun and laughter and the enjoyments of life. Though throughout the book we have seemed to have described at great length the destructive qualities of the Child, here we must emphasize strongly that it is this Child who is the source of every person's zest and sparkle, creativity, humor, sexual pleasure, delight, optimism, and ability to love. The Child is the flower and charm of the personality, enhancing the Adult with all of his happy, positive feelings. The Child is the one who engages with other people and gives us the flow of feelings without which we are not truly alive.

We *must* cherish and nurture the Child so we can enjoy all of the Child's delightful qualities. We must help make him relaxed and free so he will lend the Adult his joyous spirit. But most of all, we must give him what he so desperately needs so that we free him from his destructive impulses.

What the Child Needs from the Adult

What the Child needs and craves is what every child needs, what he wanted as a child and still wants. He wants to be paid attention to and responded to. He wants his precious and precarious self-esteem to be cherished and built up. He wants constant reassurance that he will not be harmed or destroyed or abandoned. He wants to be taken care of and approved of and understood. He wants to feel special and important. He wants to be protected. He wants freedom from responsibility. He wants permission to be joyful, encouragement to play and have fun. He wants to feel safety in expressing himself. He wants freedom from unreasoning feelings of guilt or anger. He wants everybody to give him love and approval, recognition and admiration. He wants to be cuddled and held and fussed over, and he wants not one word of criticism or scolding.

It is as if he is saying, "Tell me that you love me, very, very often; tell me that I'm special, that you'll always take care of me, because I'm little and I can't take care of myself. Tell it to me often, and if you do I'll love you and be so happy and full of fun and I'll make you happy too."

The Adult's Role

The only one to truly give the Child what he wants is the Adult. The Adult should give the Child *everything* in the way of love, nurturing, and the emotional support the Child so desperately craved and felt he did not get. The Adult should tell the Child everything he himself as a Child wanted to hear and never heard. The Adult should comfort him and reassure him when he is upset or frightened or bewildered or angry or otherwise suffering and in trouble. He should help and support the Child when he flounders and is helpless. He should set firm limits without disparaging him or humiliating him when he gets out of hand and acts irrationally. He should allow and encourage the Child's expression of all his emotions—fear, rage, anger, hurt, helplessness—without negating the Child's right to feel these or attempting to minimize them. He should be for the Child an accepting person with whom the Child can interact.

In addition, it is the role of the Adult to demonstrate with actions that he will always take care of the Child, who is so helpless and dependent. Each time the Adult succeeds in any endeavor, and each time the Adult takes over and corrects a situation which the Child has mismanaged—admitting an error, making an apology, paying an old debt—he is demonstrating to the Child with actions that he is protecting him from painful or unhappy experiences and providing him with happy and successful ones instead. This gives the Child the feeling of security he needs, and confidence in the Adult. With these feelings of security the Child will work *with* rather than against the Adult.

What the Adult is now embarking upon is a program of bringing the Child up all over again, but in a better way, and much more quickly. Using the dialogue he will help the Child uncover the unsatisfying responses he experienced early in life and replace them with satisfying responses. He will explain things just as to an actual child, in order to soothe him in his distress. He will, in effect, now become the Child's mature, loving parent. He will provide a new emotional environment: the nurturing one this Child never had and still needs.

The Adult must endeavor to assume the role of the "good-enough mother" but if he is unsure of what that entails, how will he know how to be a good parent to his Child? If he has not known how to take care of his Child before, how can he do it now, and be an Adult all at once? The answer is that he does not have to be, and need not be. No matter how unsure and shaky his Adult, almost any person can develop the insight necessary to bolster the Adult part of him and strengthen him in the Adult role. If there is even a vestige of an Adult functioning in any area, the individual can start from that point, as did the original therapy group as well as did the group of untrained women.

How the Adult Knows What to Do—Step One

The first step for the Adult is to know what the Child is thinking and feeling, and for this the Adult must get him to articulate his feelings spontaneously. Some of us may not be quite sure which feelings these are, since our Child-feelings and our Adult-feelings may be enmeshed and unseparated. The way to probe into our Child-feelings is to make a conscious effort to get in touch with them, and to become aware of them. Each of us is familiar with the monologue going on inside his head, which is so much a part of us that we are often not completely aware that it is there. Become aware of this monologue; this is the Child talking and talking and talking, with no one to listen to him or respond to him.

Become very conscious of what he is saying, for these are your Child-feelings. After a while you will realize that he talks on two levels. He reacts to things which upset him on an immediate basis —a foreground upsetness—and in these cases we know the reasons we are upset: being put down by someone, losing a job, mismanaging a relationship. But the Child is also always emitting background "static," sometimes in actual words, sometimes in feelings of discontent, or anxiety, or depression, or some other negative feelings— feelings which can be quite pronounced or which can be somewhat vague.

For the moment, put aside the day-to-day kinds of problems which can upset you. Concentrate instead on these background feelings in your attempt to gain some of the insight your Adult will need in responding to your Child and your Child's problems.

There are personality types which result from specific kinds of child rearing. If you listen closely, the deep feelings of your Child will reveal themselves. Your Child may express feelings you have carried inside you and suffered from all your life, in greater or lesser degree.

The following is an example of one type of distressed Child, what he feels, and how a mature Adult would handle him.

The Guilt-Ridden Child—An Example

Most probably this child had parents who consistently made him feel guilty in one way or another. Their attitudes and feelings toward him might have been expressed in remarks like:

"Get over here! Don't you know how to act? You never do anything right, you rotten kid! I'll get a heart attack from you! God will punish you yet!"

Much more goes into creating a guilt-ridden child, of course: things which he may have no control over, like death or divorce, but which he may *think* are his fault; and normal human mistakes everyone makes, like failing a test in school, or losing the change coming home from the grocer's. Except that this child is not allowed to forget them. If the parent does nothing to relieve the child of real or imagined guilts, and if he speaks and acts toward him in a way to make him always feel wrong, the result is a person who all his life carries with him feelings such as:

"I'm no good. . . . Everything I do is wrong. . . . When things go wrong, it's my fault—I just know it. I know I loused up at work last week, but I'm afraid to tell anybody. I'm really just in the way —nobody cares about me or wants me around. How can anybody love me? I would like people to like me, and I would like lots of nice clothes and things, but why should I have them? It's only for *me*, and I know I don't deserve it. I wish I could just crawl away and die."

And it goes without saying, these inner feelings permeate the thinking of the grown individual and influence his every action.

What would a strong, mature, loving Adult do and say to direct this Child out of these self-defeating feelings, and into an accepting attitude toward himself? What would a mature Adult have to feel and have to be in order to do this? If this were your Child suffering from these feelings, what would your Adult do?

These are the questions which the Individual—you—must find the answers to, so that you can help to strengthen your Adult in his task of helping the Child. For it is you, the Individual, the controlling element in the Separation Triangle, who calls the Adult part of you into play and bolsters him in his role of good parent to the Child. It is your task to visualize your Adult as he needs to be, and to establish him in his appropriate posture. This is the second step.

How the Adult Knows What to Do—Step Two

In some way—and there are many successful ways to do it—the Individual needs to find a model or pattern to emulate. For a person in therapy, the therapist, as one part of the therapy, will be providing models to help and strengthen the person as a well-functioning Adult, and will be demonstrating the actions of a well-functioning Adult for the person to adopt.

In managing and retraining his guilt-ridden Child, a well-functioning Adult would not necessarily feel within himself that he is responsible for everything that goes wrong, and so would not automatically blame himself. As an Adult he can be critical of himself, but in a constructive, nondamaging way. He will not indulge in self-punishing thoughts or actions. He feels he is entitled to be fallible, and that he does not have to spend his life under a cloud of guilt and he can be as happy and accepted as anyone else. He might say something like the following to a guilt-ridden Child:

"You're very hard on yourself. You did nothing wrong, and even if you made a stupid mistake, you're only five years old and you can make a mistake. It doesn't mean you're a bad person—and if your mother told you that, she was wrong. You're a good boy, and you have a right to be happy. And I'm going to watch out for the mistakes, and you only have to have fun and not worry."

There are various other kinds of distressed Child: the angry, hostile Child who feels he wants to lash out and get even with everyone; the insecure Child, who is fearful of everything and afraid to make a decision; the inferior Child who feels he can never, ever make it. And there are many more.

The example that has been given in detail illustrates briefly the first two steps in the process: first, that of becoming aware of the feelings of the Child within, and second, providing a picture, a role model, to imitate. Of course, besides the imitation of a role model, there are several other ways in which the individual can strengthen and bolster his Adult. It should be realized that it is not the intention of this book to provide personal psychoanalytic insight to each reader, but only to provide him with a proven tool to put his insights to work for him, however he may have acquired them. But there are some things which the reader can pursue and can learn to do:

1. Help your Adult by listening to your own mature voice of reason. Make it a consistent habit to ask yourself, What is the sensible thing to do? What is the practical thing to do? If I follow this course of action will I come out ahead? Then let the Adult part of you take over and do it. Each time you allow your Adult to act in this way, you are making him stronger and making it easier for him to be adult the next time.

2. Keep telling yourself over and over again, I am stronger than I know; I am smarter than I know. I may not like what is happening but I can manage as an Adult.

3. Adopt a role model, or several role models, successful adults whom you admire.

4. Observe good parents in action, and approach your Child in the same way. Observe their consistently loving, supportive attitude and see what they do when a little boy or girl of theirs is insecure or troubled.

5. When faced with a problem, achieve some objectivity by asking yourself what advice you would give to a dear friend, and act on it.

6. Read the self-help books.

7. Practice seeing your Adult as you would like him to be; give yourself strong positive suggestion.

8. Above all, maintain the motivation and determination to activate the Adult and to nurture the Child. Once even a germ of motivation is there, pounce on it with the separation and the dialogue.

With practice and resolution, almost any person will profit, at least on the conscious day-to-day level. If you feel you have deeper problems which you do not have the insight to handle well enough, you may wish to seek professional help. For some this may be advisable, and in conjunction with the Separation technique will speed you toward the goal of maturity and emotional freedom.

How the Adult Knows What to Do—Step Three

The final step in the process is the dialogue; it is the overt means by which the Child is kept separated and by which the Adult stays in control. The Child is treacherous and sabotaging, and any moment that the Adult is unguarded the Child in a split second will take over, overwhelm, and sabotage the Adult. This is why the Individual must keep the Child outside, where the Adult can see him, get in touch with his feelings, talk to him, and reassure him.

Keeping the dialogue alive will help the Individual stay in close touch with the maturing process of the Adult part of him, and with the retraining process of the Child.

The Individual can keep the dialogue alive in several ways:

1. The Individual should hold a dialogue daily, preferably at the same time and place. The Adult (Big) should greet the Child (Little), put him into a happy mood, promise him a good day, and if necessary lead him into responding and in this way lift his mood.

2. It is preferable to write the dialogues, especially at the beginning. This provides a discipline, and also allows the Individual to monitor the dialogue to see that he is doing it properly. In the beginning they may be somewhat lengthy, and this is usual. Sometimes the Child needs to talk and talk. Later the dialogues will be telescoped and direct. Writing the dialogues also establishes skill in doing them so that dialogues will come more easily, and be more productive.

3. The quality of the dialogue should be kept light and gamelike, to reinforce for the Child the feeling that everything will be all right, and also reinforce his feeling of confidence in the strength and capability of the Adult.

Be prepared for this: You will not always be able to establish a dialogue, and there will be periods of silence when you, the Individual, will not be in touch with either the Child or the Adult, or they with each other. This is the unseparated condition in the Individual who is trying to become more mature, and is a sign that no progress is taking place. By this resistance the Individual is showing that he is not motivated to change. In the words of one patient, "Separating is tantamount to being fully mature. It is making the decision to become adult. The more often we are separated, the closer we are to being fully mature. It is the decision to really love yourself and to take proper care of yourself. It's keeping in touch with the will to succeed."

The separation does not happen all at once, because most people make some progress, then fall back, then make progress again, so that most people are separated at some times and not separated at others.

The goal of Separation Therapy is that the person function on a mature level at all times, and this is possible. The tool of Separation Therapy is the dialogue, by means of which we achieve that goal.

8

The Dialogue, with Examples

The reader will see that in the following dialogues all the insights acquired up to this time come together. Through the dialogues the technique is clarified, and the Individual is able to see how weak or how strong the Adult is. He can see to what degree the overpowering Child is taking over the role of the Adult, and he can watch Big grow in strength and stature to properly take care of Little, who is so often in trouble and out of control.

These dialogues have been submitted by members of the original Monday Night Group, and by others with whom the Separation technique was discussed. The reader will see that in the beginning the dialogues are often incorrect because there is an exchange of roles between Big and Little, Big acting weak and Little strong, thus weakening the position of each.

The reader will also see that with continued practice both Big and Little become sharply defined and separated; and then, and only then, are they able to operate autonomously in their respective roles.

Dialogue #37

In which the roles of Little and Big are reversed

The following is an example of an incorrect dialogue in which Big and Little are not separated and clearly defined. They seem to be swapping roles. This often happens when one begins the technique. The reader will see that the Adult, who should be strong, appears to be weak and needy. He is permitting the Child to give him advice and help, which a child five years old is unable to give. In the process the Adult is wiped out by a weak, overwhelming Child.

    BIG: I could have gotten angry at Ethel today.

LITTLE: Yes, but lucky for you she wasn't there on time.

    BIG: Yes. She asked me to pick her up at the movie at about four P.M. Then it turned out the movie ended at four fifty. I knew then that I couldn't go to the gym, because I had to pick her up and wouldn't have enough time to do both. And I was furious.

LITTLE: If you had been on top of the situation, you would have realized that "about four" was vague. You could have checked the movie schedule yourself and found out exactly when the picture ended and when you had to pick her up. It's hard for you to do anything right. You should be more aware. Why don't you try harder?

[Therapist's comment: Little is acting like the adult and giving advice. Since he is to be thought of as not more than five, this is impossible, and cannot be permitted. The Child must stay a child, and the Adult should function as the mature, capable decision maker.]

Dialogue #38

In which Little is expressing anger by becoming emotionally flat

Mrs. B, who has been doing very well with the Separation technique, suddenly feels flat and withdrawn and does not know why. She turns to her Little and carries on a dialogue with her in which Little reveals what is causing Big to feel flat. As soon as she understands it, she is able to figure out what to do:

BIG: You seem so angry, Little.

LITTLE: I don't like Helene.

BIG: I didn't know you felt that way about her. Why don't you like her?

LITTLE: She's always complaining. She never has anything nice to say. It's better when she comes in later. When she's there I get angry. Then there is Florence, who is always wiping you and me out like we're nothing. Who does she think she is? She can't handle people the way you do. She undermines you and me all the time, and I hate her for it.

BIG: You're right, but I didn't realize that these were the things that were making me feel so low. I am going to have to speak to Florence in a more matter-of-fact, adult way. I can't allow you, Little, to speak to her in a voice that is always trying to please her. I have to do my job. I do not have to put myself out to constantly please her. Maybe her Little Girl is jealous of me because I am really doing a very competent job. I have to put every effort into this now. I am glad you told me how you feel, for now I know what to work on, and I can manage.

[Therapist's comment: Big (the Adult) was feeling flat because at this point her Child was feeling angry. Since they were not separated from each other, Big had taken in and was feeling the anger without being in touch with the cause of the feeling. This caused her to withdraw and feel flat. She was able to get in touch with these angry feelings only when she separated the Child from herself. The Child was then able to reveal real emotions and true feelings.]

Dialogue #39

In which Little begins to express feelings of anger

BIG: What's the matter, Little?

LITTLE: I'm angry. When that Dotty opens her mouth, I can't stand her.

BIG: I bet you are angry. Do you want to tell me how angry you are?

LITTLE: I sure do. I wish she'd get sick and go home and drop dead. She always makes me feel stupid.

BIG: I know how you feel.

[Therapist's comment: At this point, Big should help Little release her angry feelings, but Big is cutting her off too soon. It is important that Little be encouraged to release bottled-up, angry feelings. Big knows how Little feels too soon.]

BIG: You must understand that it is my job to cope with all problems. I may not like it, but I know I have to cope with it, not you. You are only five years old and can't solve problems. *You just keep giving me your feelings. I want to know how you feel at all times.* The only way I will know is if you keep telling me, and you can help me in this way.

LITTLE: You are saying that I must tell you how I feel at all times, and that you will work on the problems because you are the Adult. I like that idea. But you forget about me so much of the time, and I get lonely.

BIG: Keep reminding me that I am neglecting you and not giving you the love you want from me, because I do love you. You are really a good kid, and I want you to love me.

LITTLE: I will love you if you are good to me. Take me playing tennis with you. I want to have fun, too.

BIG: I am really going to try to remember. If I don't, remind me— please.

Dialogue #40

In which Little reveals her jealous feelings to Big

BIG: What's the matter, Little? You look like you're ready for a fight.

LITTLE: I am. I'm furious at Mary because she ignores me and pays attention to all your friends.

BIG: Why are you so angry?

LITTLE: I'm jealous. I want her to just pay attention to me.

BIG: I never knew you were the least bit jealous. This is news to me.

LITTLE: Well, I *am*! I hate them all, and I want Mary to like me *best*!

BIG: Is that why you have been acting so angry and feeling unhappy?

LITTLE: Yes, and I want you to know I am jealous! And I want you to like me even if I am.

BIG: Nothing's wrong with being jealous, and I love you no matter what you say or feel.

This was a person who constantly protested that there was not a jealous bone in her body, and it was quite a revelation to her to have Little give her this spontaneous and honest feeling.

After realizing that she was capable of jealousy, she became more aware, stayed with it, and was better able to manage her relationship.

Dialogue #41

In which the child who never learned is being encouraged to play

This adult was deprived as a child. She never had a childhood in which she learned how to play. She was given too much responsibility at too early an age. Big, aware of this, is trying to help her become a happier, more playful child.

BIG: Little Sue, I love you.

LITTLE: Why don't you take care of me? You make me work too hard and you never let me play. I really hate you when you work, work, work. You are just a stick-in-the-mud. You never, never play and you never, never let me play. I really hate you when you act that way.

BIG: Little Sue, I am sorry you feel that way, but certain things have to get done and while I am working you can stay right near me and play. I have a feeling that you do not know how to play, and if you can wait just a few minutes I will teach you and play with you. If you let yourself go, I think you will naturally pick up play. Don't be afraid. No one will hurt you. Reach out—the rewards are worth it. Anything you do is O.K. I will not laugh at you or call you silly. I love you, and anything you do is good. As a matter of fact, anything you do is better than good. It is great because you did it. Try, Little. It is worth it. Try and remember you will no longer be criticized or put down in any way. I love you, and anything you do will be all right with me. You are a good little girl, and once you get started I know you will be a happy, loving little girl. I love you.

LITTLE: I love you, too.

Dialogue #42

In which Big puts limits on Little

Little tells Big exactly what she is feeling, wanting something she can't have. Big puts limits on her, but gently and lovingly, without scolding. She will do this as often as necessary until Little accepts the fact that she can't always have everything her way all the time.

BIG: What's wrong?

LITTLE: I'm angry.

BIG: Why?

LITTLE: I have a stomachache, because you promised to have fun today and again you broke a promise.

BIG: So now you are punishing me. [Little is angry, and punishes Big by giving her a stomachache.]

LITTLE: Also, I was jealous.

BIG: I do understand, and I knew it before I spoke to you, but I couldn't help myself. Today I did get up extra early. I had so much to do, and I wanted to take care of the plants. Remember when you used to walk around Gramercy Park and see books and plants in the windows? Now we have our own, and I love them. I know I promised you fun and you shall have it, but *you have to learn that you can't do everything you want to do, because at times there are other things that I have to do first.*

LITTLE: But it frustrates me again, and I am jealous.

BIG: I know it frustrates you, but don't be jealous. I love you dearly, and I want you to know it.

LITTLE: So now what, with work and no time for the house or getting things in order or having fun, just being tired, what about me?

BIG: O.K., I promised a fun day, and because I couldn't do it doesn't mean I don't love you. We'll try for fun tomorrow, even on the job. If you stay with me, you and I can have fun like we used to.

LITTLE: O.K., I'll try. But remember me.

BIG: I'll really try, so remind me when I forget.

LITTLE: Please let me know you're there and help me. I need your help.

BIG: O.K., I will. But I want you to remember that I'm here.

Dialogue #43

In which Little shows that she fears men and sex

This is a dialogue in which Big is very much aware of her overpowering father, for whom she had always felt obliged to be a good girl. She has problems relating to men, especially when they seem strong or demanding. For this reason she has problems involving sex, of which she is afraid.

Big is showing a lot of insight and relieving Little of her fears by reassuring her that she will always be taken care of by Big, and by telling her that every man she goes out with is not her overpowering father. This separation is helping Big as well as Little.

BIG: You were so nervous today, and agitated. Why?

LITTLE: I feel mixed up about John and Tom.

BIG: What are you mixed up about?

LITTLE: I like John and I don't want to lose him, and yet I don't want to spend all my time with him. He is a special guy and super nice, but I want to have fun and run around and meet new people and be with my friends.

BIG: You have a right to feel that way. I understand. You don't have to have it on his terms only. You can do as you please.

LITTLE: I'm afraid I'll lose him if I'm independent. I feel I don't have a right to feel this way, and I have to do it all his way. Just like with my daddy. I had to do it all his way or I'd lose his love. When I started to be independent, he was angry and didn't accept me.

BIG: That made you feel terrible and insecure, didn't it?

LITTLE: Yes. I needed his love, and I never felt I could be a whole person and do what was good for me and still be loved.

BIG: John isn't your daddy. Your daddy didn't want sex with you. He only wanted to be boss, and you want someone who will let you be you. You have a right to be you and do what is good for you. You might lose him and you might not, but what is most important is that you do what is right for you. That you be happy is the most important thing in the world to me.

LITTLE: I don't like going to bed with John. I like sex, but when someone expects it or demands it, it frightens me.

139

BIG: Why does it frighten you?

LITTLE: I feel closed in, and that I don't have a choice. Like my daddy, always chasing me and after me. My head hurts just thinking about it. I hate my father. I hate him—I hate him. He was always after me, making me feel closed in and not whole, and without choice. He always treated me as if I was his girlfriend instead of his daughter. I hate him, and I'm afraid of sex because of him.

BIG: When a man wants to have sex with you, it feels like it's your father chasing you, doesn't it?

LITTLE: Yes. It makes me feel I have to run to protect myself.

BIG: Protect yourself from what?

LITTLE: Protect myself from my father enveloping me and suffocating me. He suffocated me, wiped me out, didn't treat me as if I was whole but as if I was an object that he could push around and use as his plaything. I always had to do things his way, and be at his side. I hate him.

BIG: I don't blame you for hating him. He wasn't good for you. He made you afraid of sex and men, and made you feel that all a man wanted from you was to own you and have sex, and that you had no right to be your own person. He was a lousy father.

LITTLE: I don't want to feel this way anymore. I want to enjoy sex, but only when I have sex casually can I relax. Then I feel free.

BIG: How does it feel on a sustained basis?

LITTLE: I feel I have to give when I don't feel like it. Also I feel hemmed in.

BIG: Sex feels nice, though. Your body feels alive and you feel womanly. You can have sex and feel free to say yes or no and be your own person. With Robert you had no choice. Sex was on his terms only. Every night everything was on his terms only, just like your father. But it doesn't have to be that way. I think it's good with John. You like him, but you are letting him know you want to be free and do what is good for you. You deserve to feel this way and do what is good for you.

LITTLE: I don't feel I deserve that choice.

BIG: But you do deserve the choice. You are very special, and you deserve to be happy and follow your instincts and have fun. You lived before without John and you can live without him again, but most important is that you do what is right for you. I love you and

I want you to be a happy little girl who has fun, lots of fun, and the hell with the rest. You don't have to be available at someone else's whim or need. Your need comes first. Your needs come first.

LITTLE: You have to keep telling me that.

BIG: I will. I will help you till you believe me and believe that you deserve the best, and that you come first with me always. I love you.

LITTLE: I feel a little better. I was also upset about Tom. He frightened me.

BIG: Why did he frighten you?

LITTLE: He is so strong. I'm afraid of being swallowed up—like with my daddy. He asks a lot and is powerful, and I'm also feeling that I have to do things his way, and it scares me and I don't like it.

BIG: He is strong, but I'm strong too. If he asks too much I will say no for you, and I will ask for what you want. I'm strong and I'll take care of you. You had such a good time on Sunday. No reason to run away from it. I'll take care of you and I'm strong for you. You have the fun, like on Sunday, and I'll be strong for you. It's an experiment—let's try it.

LITTLE: O.K. But also, with him I don't feel I have a choice. I feel that I have to be available for him when he wants it, on his terms, and I don't like it.

BIG: He would like that, but you don't have to do anything of the sort. I'm strong, and I'm taking care of you and your needs, and will ask for you and say no for you, and you just enjoy the fun part. Maybe he is demanding. I will see and then decide for you. But meantime, just have fun. He is a lot of fun, isn't he?

LITTLE: Yes, he is. I had a lot of fun with him, and he can dance, and I want to have fun with him. [The separated Child is the fun-loving, exciting part of the personality.]

BIG: If he calls, you can have fun and I'll be watching over you. He can't swallow you up, because I'm here watching. You do have a choice. You can do what is good for you, not him. I have to take care of *you* first, not him or anyone else. You are the most important little girl in the world to me, and your happiness comes first. I love you. You deserve to feel happy and free and do what makes you happy. You deserve to be who you are, and not wait around and always be available. You are too special.

LITTLE: I feel good, and I feel more relaxed. You have to keep telling me all this. This is new for me. I need your love a lot, and your help.

BIG: I know you need me, and I will help you all your life. I'm your best friend and I love you. *You will tell me all your feelings, and I will be here to listen to all you feel and to help you.* I am strong and with you all the time, taking care of you.

LITTLE: What a relief. I feel so much better. All those worries—you will take care of them for me?

BIG: Yes. *All those worries are mine, not yours. You just have fun and I will take care of all the problems.* They are for me to handle, and you just have a good time and know that I am taking care of you and love you. *You just tell me what you feel, and your complaints and worries, so I can help you and you can have fun.*

LITTLE: I love you and I need you. You make me happy. You are really the only one who can make me happy. When you are taking care of me, I'm the happiest . . . and I want to be happier all the time.

BIG: Yes. When you know that I'm with you you feel secure and loved and protected. Much better than if someone else is doing it. Turn always to me, and I will always help you and love you. You've always waited passively for men to give you what you want and it made you unhappy. *Now I'm going to do what is right for you and take care of you, and be more independent. I want to be the chooser, and do what's right for you and me.* [Big is separating from Little, loving her, and assuming responsibility as an Adult for taking care of her.]

Dialogue #44

In which Little is feeling guilty and insecure about having had a sexual experience

Little is feeling very guilty and insecure and afraid because she thinks she has done the wrong thing by having had sex with Tom, whom she had just met.

The reader will see that Big is assuming the responsibility for having made the decision to do what she did. In this way, Big is relieving Little of her fears and feelings of guilt.

LITTLE: Why did you let me go to bed with him last night? I just wanted to be his friend. Now how can I face him again? I'm scared. I'm dirty.

BIG: Why do you feel like dirt?

LITTLE: I just followed my instincts. I shouldn't have done it.

BIG: I know how you feel, but to me you are really O.K., and you did nothing wrong. I still love you, and you didn't make the decision last night. I did—and I knew what I was doing.

LITTLE: I bet he thinks I'm awful. What will I do if he doesn't call again?

BIG: I can't promise you that he will call again; I hope he does. But if he doesn't, I don't have to like it but I will be able to manage. I can manage and make today a good day for you and me. Remember, it is up to me to take care of you. You are only four years old.

LITTLE: I feel a little better, and thanks for taking care of me. I love you.

BIG: I love you too.

LITTLE: I enjoyed last night so much. I had such a good time with him. He said I was so warm and loving. I liked that. But I should have said something smart when I left . . . something womanly. Oh, hell. I want my mommy to take care of me and love me.

BIG: I understand your feelings, honey. But remember, I make all the decisions, and I am the one to say smart womanly things, not you. I will always take care of you. I am smarter and stronger than you imagine. Last night when I left his house it was up to me to say something—the right things—because you are too young to handle such a situation. In the future I just have to be more aware. But I will make the decision as to what to do as time goes on. I'll see if he calls.

LITTLE: And I am so afraid that he won't like me anymore. And I don't want that to happen. I like him and I want him to like me, too. And I did have a good time with him.

BIG: I am glad that you had a good time. You must remember the nice feelings you had there, and I will make all decisions about the future with him. You know I can. Today I will work on making this a good day for you and me, because I am in control and I love you.

Dialogue #45

In which Little expresses indecision and fear

Little is giving Big her honest feelings. And Big, separated from Little, is giving her love and emotional security. She reassures her that the problem belongs to Big to work through, not to Little.

BIG: Well, how are you tonight, Little?

LITTLE: I'm so excited that Tom called again. I was so afraid he wouldn't call after last time. I want him to hold me—but what if he doesn't want to? I want him to think I'm special. I really like him a lot. I loved it when his body touched mine, especially when he touched my face. I really want to crawl into bed with him and just lie next to him. I want to look beautiful, and I'm still a little frightened after last time. How should I act? What will I say? Maybe I shouldn't go at all.

BIG: I know how you're feeling, and I feel the same way sometimes. But even if I get scared and don't like what might happen, I will be able to cope with it. You will come with me and have fun, and I will be able to manage whatever happens. I will be in control and play it by ear. I am a woman, calm and cool, and I will think things through before I make any decisions. I am gambling with Tom, but I have made a decision to just enjoy the situation. It is a good experience for me, and I want to be his friend and enjoy every minute of the relationship.

LITTLE: I like to hear you talk like that. You make me feel good.

Dialogue #46

In which Little is feeling unloved and deprived

Big nurtures her Child by trying to get in touch with a need that Little is experiencing at a particular time. Since Little is the separated part of Big, in giving love and reassurance to her, Big is really nurturing herself at the same time.

BIG: You really had a bad day today. Lots of things were bothering you. Tell me about it.

LITTLE: I have always had such a hard time with Sarah. She cuts me off all the time when I talk to her. She wants her own way and is always Number One. I hate her. I want to be Number One and she won't let me. I hate her, and I could have killed her today.

BIG: Why does she make you feel all wiped out?

LITTLE: I want her to mother me like everyone else. I want her to love me and coddle me. My sister always wiped me out and put me down and never made me feel special. Sarah treats me the same way.

BIG: You really want your sister to love you. It's too bad you didn't have a sister who made you feel special. It would have been nice, and it would have been nice if you had had a loving father and mother. But you weren't that lucky. But now you are lucky. You have me and I love you and I think you are special, so you can live without your sister's love.

LITTLE: Yes I can, but I still want to be Number One wherever I am and with everyone. I was Number One with my father against my sister, and I still need to be Number One. I want love and acceptance from everyone, and I don't feel as if I am getting it. It makes me feel bad.

BIG: I want you to believe that I feel you are special and lovable. You don't need love from everyone when you can get it from me—not so much anyway. You will always be unhappy if you look for it and wait for it. You have me and I love you. I don't want you to be an unhappy little girl. I want to make you a happy little girl, my Little Girl who believes she is my special little girl. I love you, and as long as you believe my love for you, you won't need so much from everyone else. I love you.

LITTLE: I want to believe you. I am tired of feeling rotten. I don't want to need people so much. I want to feel your love. I want to feel good. *I don't want to wait for permission to feel good anymore.* I want you to take care of me.

BIG: You can depend on me. I want you to. When you believe that I love you and that I think you are special, you won't care so much what others think. I love you and I will make you feel secure. As an adult, I will love you and always take care of you. I want you to share all your feelings with me, and I will always be there to have fun with you and to help you when you are in trouble. *I will take care of all your troubles and you can relax.*

LITTLE: You make me feel so good. I know you will always take care of me, and I love you so much too.

Dialogue #47

In which Little is feeling sorry for herself

In this dialogue Big is replacing the feelings of a self-pitying Child with encouragement and love. She does this by showing her that there is a better way to get love than by crying and manipulating people so they give her what she considers love by feeling sorry for her.

BIG: How do you feel now? You seem a little droopy. Why?

LITTLE: I feel like a little girl with all these big people around me, and I'm not in control of things around me.

BIG: You are a little girl, and you are forgetting that you aren't supposed to be in control. I am in control of things around you. You are just a little girl with big people around, but I am a big person in charge and taking care of my Little Girl, you. I love you, and you don't have to do any worrying. You just have fun, and I will take care of things for you. I'm your best friend, remember? I love you. Tonight you are going to have so much fun. You are going dancing —which you love to do.

LITTLE: I don't feel good about tonight. I'm afraid I won't have a good time. I won't have anyone to dance with, and I don't feel I have the right to have fun tonight.

BIG: Why don't you feel you have the right to have fun?

LITTLE: It's almost like a bad-luck sign. If I keep on having fun, something will happen to me.

BIG: What will happen to you?

LITTLE: If I keep on having fun and dancing and feeling good I will have nothing to feel sorry for myself about, and I won't know what to do then. I am so used to feeling sorry for myself. I don't know how else to feel. I am afraid to give it up. I feel loved in a strange way when I feel sorry for myself.

146

BIG: I love you when you don't feel sorry for yourself. I love you all the time. You can get love when I am strong and you are happy. People will love you, and most of all you will be happier not begging for it. I will give you all the love you need, and I will ask for it for you. You were always so used to crying for sympathy to get love. That is all you know, and you are afraid to change.

LITTLE: That's right. I need people to love me so much, and I got a lot of love that way. And I don't want to give the love up, so I cry for sympathy.

BIG: You won't give the love up. There is just a better and newer way to get love. First, I will give you all the love you need, as much as you want and need. Second, I will ask for it from other people for you. In this way you will not be wiped out in the process, and you will know how much I love you. It is a much better and healthier way. You no longer have to beg and wait. I love you.

LITTLE: O.K. I'll try it with you. Keep loving me.

Dialogue #48

In which Big gives love and puts limits on Little

This is a good example of how Big gives to a very needy Child the kind of love and nurturing that is meant in the Separation technique. Big is also gently putting limits on Little by giving her love but letting her know she cannot have everything she wants on her terms.

LITTLE: I feel very low. I feel washed out and flat, and I don't like it. I feel like a little-bitty girl, and I want you to put your arms around me and cuddle me and love me like a mommy I never had. I feel very alone, and all I want is to be in your arms like a little baby and you will make everything all right. But I am scared.

BIG: Why are you so scared?

LITTLE: I need love so much.

BIG: I know you need a lot of love and cuddling. You need good friends and people to love you—but it is not good for you to go on feeling this way. You are only hurting yourself.

LITTLE: I know I am hurting myself, but I can't help myself.

BIG: It's no good to feel sorry for yourself. Hell, you've only got one life to live—and you deserve a good life. So come on, sing a song, and then I'll call somebody up and I'll take you to have some fun.

Dialogue #49

In which the Child expresses deep needs to be taken care of, loved, and accepted

Little is expressing feelings of needing to be approved of and loved. She also feels extremely helpless and is asking Big to take care of her. Many people have these feelings without being conscious of them. Though they may not be expressed in words, these needs come out in actions which are often not to the best interests of the individual.

In this dialogue, Little is crying out to be taken care of and approved of and loved. Big is able to satisfy these emotional needs of the babyish Child only because the Child and the Adult are separated and the Adult is able to be mature and objective. This kind of dialogue may have to be repeated often until Little feels that she is worthy of love and acceptance. When the Adult assumes the responsibility of his Little, he is really assuming the responsibility for himself.

LITTLE: I want you to take care of me always. Never leave me alone. Keep me with you all the time, and keep showing me that you know I am there.

BIG: I'm glad you told me how you feel, because now that I know what you want, I will give it to you.

LITTLE: I'm little. I can't take care of myself. I need you to do that.

BIG: (Smilingly says) Don't worry. You have me. You will never be alone again, and I will always take care of you. I'll be good to you, and I will love you.

LITTLE: And I'll love you too.

BIG: That makes me very happy.

In this process the Adult grows, is able to assume more and more responsibility for her Little, who is always with her (though separated and outside of her). This process strengthens the Adult.

Dialogue #50

In which Big helps Little when she is suffering from old childhood fears

BIG: Why are you so upset?

LITTLE: Because I don't want to see your family today. I hate them. They're no good, and hostile and ignorant. I don't want to be with them. I'm afraid that you will slip back to being like them. I'm afraid, and I want to go home.

[Therapist's comment: Little is expressing fear that Big will regress to the point where she will let her family upset her, as they have always done in the past. Big reassures her that she, Little, has nothing to fear, and that Big will continue to handle this problem and protect her. Because Big and Little are separated from each other, Big is able to do this.]

BIG: I understand everything you're feeling, and I am only here to observe these people and do what will benefit me. Don't worry. I can handle their hostility. . . . And though I started on the ground with these people, how lucky you and I are that I have learned so much and have outgrown them. You and I will never go back. I will not permit that to happen. It was only when you needed them that they hurt you; but you don't need them anymore so they can't hurt you. I will take you back to Westchester, to your own surroundings. Be patient, because everything I do will benefit you.

Dialogue #51

In which the Child with a poor self-image is helped to feel better about herself

What the Adult is saying to the Child may be extremely obvious and simple. But it is still true, and the Child seems to need to hear it. Therefore it is most important to express it out loud, so that what may not be too strong a feeling is reinforced for both the Child and the Adult.

The following is a good example in which the Adult gives to her nontrusting Little the emotional support she needs, in an effort to change Little's self-image.

BIG: I love you.

LITTLE: I don't believe you.

BIG: I don't blame you for not trusting me. But you can trust me, because now that I know what you want, it will be easy for me to give it to you.

LITTLE: Why will it be easy now?

BIG: Because I love you. I think you are an adorable little girl, and I love you more than I can say.

LITTLE: How can you love me? I'm such a rotten kid.

BIG: You're not rotten. You were just misunderstood. Every time you wanted to show feelings, they said you were rotten. But you have to show feelings. Let's forget about *them*. They were really stupid. Just remember that I love you and that I will always take care of you.

LITTLE: I don't believe it.

BIG: I don't blame you for not believing me. But have faith in me. I am big and I am strong, and I will take care of you—and I want to, because I love you.

LITTLE: That makes me feel good, and I love you too.

CASE HISTORY

Jack

When Jack came into treatment, he was worried about his relationships with people—especially his bosses and customers, with whom he was always angry and with whom he fought constantly. His conduct at home with his wife and their new daughter was likewise destructive. He said he was unable to make the slightest decision, that people were always trying to take advantage of him, and that he felt completely immobilized.

Jack's early childhood showed great deprivation in all areas. He was extremely dependent on his mother and her moods. He felt that his mother, whom he considered the strength of the family, rejected and reduced him in every possible way. It seemed to him that she also belittled his father and his brothers. Jack withdrew and lived in a fantasy world of his own, unable and afraid to try. Although bright, he never worked up to his capacity. Very little premium was placed on education in his family, and when he became valedictorian of his high-school graduation class, his mother made nothing of it. He was also discouraged from studying further.

While he was an actor, he met his wife. He made no money as an actor, but hoped he would catch on. This attitude became more unrealistic, since he now had his daughter and wife to support. Because he had no skills, he was forced to work at menial jobs. But his thoughts were constantly on acting. He said that at this time he was passive, incapable of loving, and that he relied completely on his wife. His dependency needs were great.

He had a great need to "continually prove something to everybody," and lived in constant fear of criticism by others. He was always on the defensive. He was extremely hostile, and afraid to feel. He felt that this was tied up with his feelings of inadequacy and sense of worthlessness. He absolutely could not stand being rejected.

As a child he got no love from his parents. "I was ashamed, embarrassed by, and afraid of them, especially my mother. My brothers rejected me. When the one I hated most died, I had guilt feelings because I felt that I had wished it on him. I don't trust anyone, and I have no faith in anyone." Jack was always waiting for someone to do for him. Meanwhile, when not working, he slept his time away. At this point he was an immature, narcissistic, passive-aggressive man who was seeking help, through therapy, in an effort to mobilize himself to achieve some vocational success. But what he really wanted was someone to do it for him.

In time Jack began to develop some understanding, but he continued to be discouraged easily. He learned that he had a tendency to run away by sleeping and withdrawing into silence and into his own little world. He understood that at such times his tendency was to become completely unaware of his surroundings. He began to recognize his fears. "I am able to see more clearly the things that were so distorted for me. I understand my fear of bosses and people in authority. It is a fear that they will reject me by finding fault as my mother did. Why am I so upset when I feel that people are rejecting me?" He was encouraged to talk in this area, and he developed some insight. He began to talk about his mother, but still with inappropriate emotions. He expressed angry words but with no feelings.

"I was afraid of my parents and unable to express my feelings with them, so I never got what I wanted from them. I had no love in my childhood. I felt lonely and abandoned, especially by my mother, who cut off all my feelings. Even my brothers rejected me. How could I love? I'm afraid of my feelings. I have always been a clown like my father—at my own expense."

Jack gradually began to express feelings of trust toward his therapist. He began to express real feelings toward those with whom he came in contact. He understood his resentment of anyone in authority, and he became much more aware of himself, his feelings, and his manipulations for defeat. His hostilities came out slowly, but there appeared to be progress in his self-understanding, self-control, and relationships with other people. He seemed to be maturing. This also manifested itself in his relationship with his wife, whom he had formerly terrorized in a most sadistic way. He began to understand the conflicts he felt when he had to put out any real effort.

He became aware of his feelings of unworthiness and his will to fail. He talked more freely, releasing more hostility, not only toward his mother but also toward his therapist, Mrs. Kirsten. He continued to be aware of his feelings. He recognized his reaction to frustration and was able to verbalize it. He also showed increased capacity for releasing anger.

He worked through his conflicts about the middle-class values of the area in which he now lived. He reached out and related to the community. He joined the church and produced plays, for which he received much recognition.

Jack's feelings toward his wife began to change. Instead of demanding and wanting to "take" all the time, he was more willing to give of himself to her and to the children (he now had two), who responded beautifully. He was now able to think in terms of the needs of his family in addition to his own. "I have much more awareness of how much of what I do and think is coming from my unconscious. I always got into trouble when I thought people were critical of me. Now I don't seem to care, and I can think more clearly.

"I am amazed at myself and the way I am managing. I always felt that everything that went wrong was my fault. Now I stop and ask myself, 'How can I handle this situation?' I no longer feel that everyone is trying to take advantage of me. My feelings about money are freer. I know, now, that I don't have to prove anything to myself and to others. I try to do the best that I can do, and then try not to worry too much. I find that I am much more satisfied with myself, and for longer periods of time."

Recently, after many years of therapy, he said, "I am amazed at my ability to influence those who work for me and with me. I am amazed at my capacity to give and receive love." Jack has developed strong leadership qualities and has increased his earnings. "Since I came from the bottom of the barrel with such feelings of worthlessness, it is amazing to me that I now function with a true sense of worth, and that I am no longer dependent on anyone else. Gratified as I am by my progress over the years, through therapy, discovering and separating the Adult from the Child has increased my awareness of my behavior. It has made it easier for me to cope with the problems of living that I am faced with each day. I feel that I am smarter than anybody else, because I know something that they don't know. I now have established a friendly, loving, sympathetic relationship with myself. And even now when I regress—and I do regress—I no longer have to pay the price of punishing myself for days, because I become aware of the process instantly and put the Separation technique to work for me."

Some time ago, Jack was promoted to an executive position. Recently he was given an award for outstanding achievement at the company's annual banquet. He received this not only for his service to the company but for his service to the community as well.

Much of the success he is enjoying he attributes to his ability to keep Little separated from Big. With this technique he finds that he tries to put his Adult in control whenever he has to solve a problem, thus strengthening the Adult and making life easier for himself.

Jack/Dialogue #52

Jack's early dialogues confused the Child and the Adult. There was no real separation. Notice that Little gives advice and both talk of "we."

BIG: Little, why the hell did I commit myself to write this s——t?

LITTLE: You know why: It's important and you tend to be lazy.

BIG: I know I hate to start projects, but once I do I feel happy.

LITTLE: You feel very successful lately, don't you?

BIG: Hey, how come I'm the Adult and you sound so smart?

LITTLE: I don't know. It doesn't make sense, but I am not going to question it since it is working for me. I like myself and I feel secure—what a beautiful feeling!

BIG: It wasn't always that way, was it?

LITTLE: I refuse to think those awful negative thoughts. Up to recently I thought only negative thoughts only too easily. Now I refuse to return to that lousy, habitual person.

BIG: Hey, I could write this by hand, and I could write faster and sloppier and unhappily like I used to, and it would be more representative of me.

LITTLE: I REFUSE TO!

BIG: How the hell did we just switch roles? Now Big seems smarter and positive and Little negative. I don't know. What's more important, I don't care. I only know I will perform positive actions from now on, no matter who in me is giving the advice. I like myself both as Child and Adult. I refuse to move from that position, right?

LITTLE: RIGHTTTT! What about the money you owe?

BIG: I will pay it in time, and not suffer in the meantime.

LITTLE: What about stopping smoking and losing some weight?

BIG: I refuse to follow this trend of thought. It is making me angry, and if I pursue it I will fall into the old negative pattern. I am not going to overwhelm myself as I used to . . . used to. Past tense. Finished. Over with.

LITTLE: Big, I love you.

BIG: Little, I love you too. I will take care of you, but I insist you help me too. We will both give and we will both benefit. We are geared for real success. We feel successful; the rest is unimportant.

LITTLE: Big, take care of me.

BIG: Come on now, you are strong and successful and worthwhile.

[Therapist's comment: Little wants to be taken care of because he always remains the Little Boy and has to be taken care of, as he has no judgment.]

Jack/Dialogue #53

This is a later attempt at using the Separation technique. Jack resisted this technique for several weeks, protesting that he hated that rotten kid and didn't want to be friends with him. However, when he started he was surprised that though Little and Big were not yet separated, they were quite playful:

LITTLE: Goddam it. Three typewriters in the house and not one works properly. I'm as mad as spit, and I don't want to put up with all this stupid frustration.

BIG: You mean you'd rather remain angry and frustrated, and accomplish no more than a temper tantrum, than be rational and do something about the situation.

LITTLE: I like you, Big. Thanks for putting me on the right track. I really need your help.

BIG: My pleasure, Little. I need you too. At first you even managed to confuse me and I thought Big me was the one who was so angry.

LITTLE: I know and I'm grateful. You caught me in time before I made a mess of things. I don't mean to be deliberately disobedient. I just get carried away, and then I get so mad I don't know what I'm doing or what I want.

BIG: I know. Don't be afraid. I will always be around to rescue you when you get into trouble, so don't fret about it.

LITTLE: You mean you love me and will take care of me and nobody can hurt me?

BIG: That's exactly what I mean and you know it.

LITTLE: I know, but I love having you say it. Say it again. [Little needs constant reassurance of Big's love, since he was a most deprived child.]

BIG: I love you and I will take care of you and I won't let anyone hurt you.

LITTLE: I love you, you son of a bitch . . . NO! I mean I love you.

BIG: And I love you, pal.

LITTLE: Can we stop now? I'm tired—it's been such a busy morning.

BIG: But if you stop you will feel just as tired, if not more.

LITTLE: I know. Help me.

BIG: I just have. Now that I've disciplined you, you don't really feel tired, do you?

LITTLE: No. I feel glad that you're not letting me run the show. I don't really want to. You know it's just that I lose control and then I'm not responsible.

BIG: I know, but you've been so clever in the past that you fooled me, you little devil. I'll have to see to it now that you are not to run amok again.

LITTLE: Do you think Grace thinks we write the best dialogues of all?

BIG: Doesn't really matter, does it?

LITTLE: No, but it would sure be nice.

BIG: Why don't we just do our own thing and not be concerned with what others think?

LITTLE: Damn it, you're right again!

BIG: I know, and aren't you glad now that we didn't stop writing sooner?

LITTLE: Yes! Yes! Yes!

BIG: Good, because we will stop now. It's time to leave.

In discussing Separation Therapy in the group, Jack made the following remarks:

1. The Adult asks for what it wants. The Child cries for it.

2. The unseparated Adult isn't able to take over and be responsible for his actions.

3. The Adult must assume responsibility for his life. I have the right to do what is good for me. I am in charge and I can do for me. The Little Boy has to understand that Big makes the decisions and he, Little, is not going to be afraid because Big will take care of him and of me. When the Adult is in control, problems are more easily understood and so can be handled.

I feel so good after writing this that I really don't feel any loss at not seeing Grace today. I feel tempted to quit therapy. I am actually looking forward to the summer and not seeing Grace, so that I can measure my strength and progress.

It takes a lot of courage for me to say this, but I feel so secure that I dare say it. I love you, Grace, but I love myself more, and that is a big statement for me to make and I feel stronger and stronger.

A Dream: Dr. Richard C. Robertiello

One of the authors had an interesting dream that he would like to share with those interested in Separation Therapy.

Dr. Robertiello was going through a period in his life in which he was experiencing more fun than he had ever had before in his life. However, because he had been a very sad child, repeatedly abandoned by his mother as a little boy, he would frequently fall into periods of sadness, loneliness, and fear of being left by loved ones, in spite of the fact that his adult life was very fulfilling.

In my dream, I was playing football on the street as part of a regular team. On this team was a tiny little boy who was apparently playing because he had a special talent for blocking kicks. As the team lined up to play, he would constantly go offside. I had to keep going after him and pulling him back to the right side of the line, or our whole team would have been penalized even if we played well. I kept after him to make sure he didn't louse up our play. And I was successful at doing this.

In my associations to the dream, I remembered that as a child, and even as a young adult, I had had considerable fun playing football on the streets of New York City. The tiny little fellow in my dream was obviously the sad Little Boy who could creep in and ruin my fun. My Adult self had to keep constant watch over this Child to prevent him from messing up my fun and my effectiveness in life in general. In this dream, I accomplished this by keeping the Child under careful control. This way the Child could play too and enjoy the game, but he did not negate the functioning of the total person.

9
Putting It All Together

It might well be asked, If it is the Individual who establishes the dialogue between the Adult and Child, and whose task it is to bolster the Adult, why can't this same Individual simply bypass the Adult, be his own strong self, and work directly with the Child? The answer is that unless the two components, the Child and the Adult, are completely outside the Individual and separated, the Individual does not have the necessary objectivity to observe and keep the Adult and Child separated and the Adult in control. The proof is that if the Individual could do this, he would have already done it! And if he has done it in some areas, it is precisely *because* he has achieved some degree of objectivity and separation.

Does this mean that the Individual must now go through the rest of his life in this separated, fragmented condition? Not at all. With practice in the technique, ultimately the Adult part of the Individual will mature to the point where he is in control practically all of the time, and the Child will have progressed to the point where he is no longer a constant threat.

However, the Child is still to be thought of as outside and separate, and if he does come in, in moments of high emotion, he is still to be under the watchful eye of the Adult. For persons who have had a distressed Child within them, it is never safe to re-incorporate the Child: It is important that the Individual continue to maintain the Child always outside and separated.

But what of the flower and charm of the personality, the zest and sparkle, all the things which a contented Child is supposed to add to the personality? If the Child is outside, how can he be part of the Individual's total self? The answer is that the Child's feelings and emotions are picked up and "caught" by the Adult in the same way that laughter or tears, being infectious, can be caught. The Adult can thoroughly enjoy and absorb the good feelings of the Child without being carried away. Then the Individual will be a total personality, integrating a mature Adult and the feelings of a happy, secure Child.

How quickly does this happen in Separation Therapy?

It happens as quickly as the Individual's degree of motivation will allow it to happen.

And it might happen more quickly than with other therapeutic techniques, because it allows whatever insight the Individual has gained about himself to be made visible and tangible. This is the unique value of Separation Therapy. Instead of an abstract, general concept of our feelings, and a vague notion of what to do with them, there is a concrete, tangible Child whom we can visualize, personified for us in the figure of the child we were. More important, there is also a concrete figure of the Adult part of us, who is every day growing more mature.

Separation Therapy works because it is so concrete.

It works because it allows the Adult to function almost as his own therapist.

It works because it allows the Individual's Adult to reprogram his Child by giving him good-enough mothering as often and as fully as the Child needs it.

It works for emotionally healthy and well-adjusted persons too, who also have a Child in them who sometimes needs help.

It works because for the first time it provides a concrete, usable technique which makes visible and tangible the process of maturing.

Index